CW01262204

RICE, MISO SOUP, PICKLES

About the Author

Yoshiharu Doi was born in Osaka in 1957 and, after graduating from the Education Faculty of Ashiya University, undertook culinary training in Switzerland, France and Osaka. He then worked as a teacher at the Masaru Doi Culinary School, before establishing *Oishiimono Kenkyūjō* (a culinary consulting group). As well as serving as Vice President of Jumonji Gakuen Women's University and spending time as a Visiting Researcher at the University of Tokyo's Research Centre for Science and Technology, Yoshiharu frequently appears on cookery programmes such as TV Asahi's *Okazu no Kukkingu* ('Japanese Homemade Recipes') and has presented NHK's *Kyō no Ryōri* ('Today's Menu') for 38 years. In 2022, he was selected for a Commissioner for Cultural Affairs Award in recognition of his outstanding achievements in the cultural field. In recent years, he has regularly taught and lectured on cookery in France and other countries. He has written numerous books, including *Ichijū Issai de Yoi to Iu Teian* ('The Proposal That One Soup and One Side Dish Is Enough', Shinchosha Publishing Co., Ltd, 2021), *Ichiju Issai de Yoi to Itarumade* ('Until I Came to Believe That One Soup and One Dish is Enough', Shinchosha Publishing Co., Ltd 2022) and *Kurashi no Tame no Ryōrigaku* ('Life Lessons in Cookery', NHK Publishing, 2021).

RICE, MISO SOUP, PICKLES

The Japanese secret to a long and happy life

By
Yoshiharu Doi

Translated from the Japanese by Gwen Clayton

yellow kite

First published in Great Britain in 2025 by Yellow Kite
An imprint of Hodder & Stoughton Limited
An Hachette UK company
The authorised representative in the EEA is Hachette Ireland, 8 Castlecourt
Centre, Dublin 15, D15 XTP3, Ireland (email: info@hbgi.ie)

1

ICHIJUISSAI DE YOI TO IU TEIAN
by Yoshiharu Doi
Copyright © Yoshiharu Doi 2016 All rights reserved
First Japanese edition published in 2016 by Graphic-sha Publishing Co., Ltd.
Japanese paperback edition published in 2021 by
SHINCHOSHA Publishing Co., Ltd.
English translation rights arranged with SHINCHOSHA Publishing Co., Ltd.
Through Japan UNI Agency, Inc., Tokyo and DAVID LUXTON ASSOCIATES, London
Translation Copyright © Gwen Clayton 2025

Text design by Goldust Design
Noodle, bowl and bun vectors © supanut piyakanont/Shutterstock.com
Chopsticks icon © UnderhilStudio/Shutterstock.com
Photograph on page 251 © Shinchosha Photography Department
All other photography © Yoshiharu Doi

The right of Yoshiharu Doi to be identified as the Author of the Work has been
asserted by him in accordance with the Copyright, Designs and Patents Act 1988.

All rights reserved. No part of this publication may be reproduced, stored
in a retrieval system, or transmitted, in any form or by any means without
the prior written permission of the publisher, nor be otherwise circulated
in any form of binding or cover other than that in which it is published and
without a similar condition being imposed on the subsequent purchaser.

A CIP catalogue record for this title is available from the British Library

Hardback ISBN 9781399741026
Trade Paperback ISBN 9781399741033
ebook ISBN 9781399741057

Typeset in Clavo Light by Hewer Text UK Ltd, Edinburgh
Printed and bound in Great Britain by Clays Ltd, Elcograf S.p.A.

Hodder & Stoughton policy is to use papers that are natural, renewable
and recyclable products and made from wood grown in sustainable
forests. The logging and manufacturing processes are expected to
conform to the environmental regulations of the country of origin.

Hodder & Stoughton Limited
Carmelite House
50 Victoria Embankment
London EC4Y 0DZ

www.yellowkitebooks.co.uk

The most important thing of all

is to live your life to the fullest.

That which you do with all your heart
is the most genuine,

And being genuine is the most beautiful
and the most precious thing of all.

Contents

A note on the translation · · · · · · · · · · · · · · · · · · · xi

One Soup and One Side Dish – Why Now?
Food is our daily life · 3
Things we never tire of eating · · · · · · · · · · · · · · · 7

A Plan for Living
Trusting your body · 15
Doing simple things with care · · · · · · · · · · · · · · · 20
A balance between extravagance and restraint · · 25
A modest life is an important preparation · · · · · · 30

Everyday Food
The significance of cooking · · · · · · · · · · · · · · · · · 37
The peace of mind that the kitchen creates · · · · · 42
To eat well is to live well · · · · · · · · · · · · · · · · · · · 46

Rice, Miso Soup, Pickles

A Soup and a Side Dish in Practice

The 'one soup and one side dish' meal model	55
The Japanese staple food: rice	57
How to prepare delicious steamed rice	58
How to cook rice cleverly in a way that fits around your daily schedule	60
Miso soup with lots of ingredients	62
A quick way to make miso soup for one person	64
All about miso	68
A miso soup that you can make straight away	72
Miso soups that you can only enjoy at certain times of year	73
One soup and one side dish in practice	82
One soup and one side dish is a style of eating	86

Those Who Cook and Those Who Eat

Professional cooking and home cooking – thoughts	95
Home cooking doesn't have to be delicious	100
The relationship between those who cook and those who eat – 'eating out'	105
The relationship between those who cook and those who eat – 'eating at home'	111
Discernment	117

The Origins of Delicious Food

Japanese culinary sensibility: think less, feel more	127
The cuisine of the Jōmon period	143
Cleanliness	151

(Re)discovering Japanese Food

Time to nurture the mind	159
The Japanese sense of beauty	165
Changes in food	169
What should I eat? What can I eat? What do I want to eat?	177
Reclaiming the model of Japanese cuisine	181

The Pleasure That Begins with One Soup and One Side Dish

Everyday pleasure	193
The pleasure of choosing and using a rice bowl	195
The pleasure when others notice your efforts, the pleasure of guessing what others have done	198
The pleasure of using a beautiful tray	204
The pleasure of sake, the pleasure of side dishes, the pleasure of the seasons (and enjoying what is in season)	207
Enjoying Japanese food culture and the pleasure of beauty	219

Japanese people who live beautifully –
  in lieu of a conclusion   223
The future of one soup and one side dish –
  on the occasion of the paperback publication   241

Afterword   Takeshi Yōrō, Anatomist,
  Philosopher and Professor Emeritus,
  University of Tokyo   252

Glossary   257

Index   265

A note on the translation

This book was originally published in Japanese with the title *Ichijū Issai de Yoi to Iu Teian*, that is, 'The Proposal That One Soup and One Side Dish Is Enough' (commonly referred to as 'One Soup and One Side Dish'). One of Yoshiharu Doi's aims in writing this book was to simplify Japanese cuisine, to reduce it to its essentials, and in so doing to make it accessible to anyone, especially young men leaving home and cooking for themselves for the first time. A Japanese home-cooked meal typically consists of rice, miso soup and various side dishes. Recent trends in social media and on television cookery shows might give the impression that, in order to be taken seriously, anyone cooking Japanese food must prepare many intricate and beautifully presented side dishes alongside rice and miso soup – the more, the better. In this book, Doi explains how, by preparing rice and seasonal pickles thoughtfully and by making miso soup with whatever raw ingredients are available, one soup and one side dish (plus rice) really is enough. Moreover, he provides a model that is simple to follow but changes with the seasons and is therefore hard to get tired of. Although the book was originally aimed at readers in Japan, Doi's philosophy as well as his descriptions are sure to appeal to anyone with an interest in Japanese food or indeed Japanese culture more generally.

Doi uses a range of ingredients available in shops in Japan which may not be available elsewhere. He also forages for some of his ingredients, which readers are not advised to do unless they are experienced foragers and familiar with their locality.

When discussing the background to and significance of home cooking, Doi takes as his standard the traditional 'nuclear' family with its traditional role allocations, but his arguments apply equally well to any home where one or more people prepare food for others to eat.

In the acknowledgements towards the end of the book, Doi refers to several people to whom he feels a debt of gratitude, usually using their surname followed by the honorific form '-san', as is typical in Japanese. Although the naming conventions we use in English are different, I decided to retain this, in order to convey something of the original.

A note on the translation

As with any translation, it seemed helpful here and there to add a few words of explanation for the English reader. There is also a glossary of Japanese food terms at the end of the book.

Gwen Clayton
London, 2025

One Soup and One Side Dish – Why Now?

今、なぜ一汁一菜か

Food is our daily life

I would like this book to be read by anyone who feels that cooking is a chore. I gather that many people find it hard to come up with a daily menu. If they work late, they might not be in the mood to cook when they get home. They prioritise matters outside the home, and put off their own needs or even neglect them entirely. They might think, 'I'll do things properly once I'm married,' but when they get immersed in their work, preparing food feels like a burden. If they live alone, cooking might be tiresome. When their children grow up and leave home, they lose the motivation to cook. There are any number of reasons why they do not or cannot cook right now.

While all this may be true, eating out on a daily basis can be problematic, both economically and nutritionally. Even with supplements, it is hard to compensate for the dietary imbalance caused, and you may be left with a sense of guilt. Our society, which people work so hard to be part of and contribute to, is one that we ourselves created; and yet, work is stressful, and fear of failure can be overwhelming. This response is understandable, but when I hear 'it's the same for everyone, that's just how it is', it feels like a small consolation. Perhaps people today lack confidence in their ability to make a living and feel anxious about the future, and while reassuring themselves that they will be fine, they still feel uncertain and unfulfilled.

I think everyone wants to have a healthy mind and a healthy body. It is hard to accomplish great things alone, but one way in which you can keep yourself healthy is by adopting a simple, healthy and sustainable menu, for example, with the idea that one soup and one side dish is enough. Why not give it a try? If it goes well, it might even become a cornerstone to support your family, your health, a beautiful lifestyle, mental fulfilment and whatever work you have to do. Over the centuries, it is through food that people have stayed alive and forged bonds with nature, society and with each other. Food is the beginning of everything: living and cooking simply go together.

If a parent knows that a child who has left home is eating properly and looking after themselves, that

Food is our daily life

is one thing less for them to worry about. Personally, I think of it as a filial duty – you should reassure your parents that you can look after yourself. Conversely, if a person knows that their ageing parent cooks every day, cleans the kitchen and looks after themselves properly, they will feel reassured and encouraged.

One soup and one side-dish is a diet based on three elements – rice, miso soup and pickles – but actually, rice and miso soup is all you need. If you need something salty, then instead of pickles, try a spoonful of miso on your rice.

Rice, Miso Soup, Pickles

What is important in daily life is where you rest your heart: to create a daily pattern which involves returning home to a comfortable place every day. Food is the pillar that supports this; the habit of coming back to something that you yourself control. This is where one soup and one side dish comes in, in other words, rice, miso soup and a side dish. The simplest version of this model is rice, miso soup and pickles.

Rice is the staple food in Japan. Miso soup is a soup in which that traditional Japanese fermented food, miso, has been dissolved. The other ingredients can be highly varied, for example, whatever vegetables one has to hand and fried or uncooked tofu. Japanese pickles are made by adding salt to vegetables and allowing them to ferment: they can be made in advance so that they are always ready to eat.

'Rice, miso soup and pickles' is not just a menu suggestion. It's a system, a philosophy and an aesthetic.

Things we never tire of eating

Surely anyone can make something as simple as this, however busy they are. All you need to do is steam some rice and make some miso soup with plenty of ingredients. You can cook it yourself.

The traditional model for Japanese cuisine, the one that will keep you fit and healthy and which you will never tire of eating, even if you have it three times a day, every day, is one soup and one side dish. If you want, you can simply decide to have this every day, for every meal. You do not need to think about it – it's not even a menu. It takes less than 10 minutes to prepare. There are even soups you can make in 5. Why not make cooking a simple Japanese meal one of the daily tasks you repeat every day, like brushing your teeth, having a shower, doing the laundry or cleaning your home? I expect everyone will be wondering whether

◗ Rice, Miso Soup, Pickles

it can be as simple as that, but it can be and it is. We have been cooking like this forever.

The amazing thing about rice and miso soup is that even if you eat them every day, you never get tired of them. What other kinds of foods could you say that about? However delicious a particular dish is, you might not want to eat it every day, day in, day out. But you can eat rice, miso soup and pickles every day without getting bored. What distinguishes food that gets boring from food that does not?

In general, processed food is so highly flavoured that it tastes delicious from the first bite. With food like this that has been deliberately and artificially flavoured, you tend to want to eat something with a different flavour immediately afterwards.

With rice, miso soup and pickles, however, there are no artificial flavours. With rice, the grains have simply been polished, added to water and steamed. Miso, which has been made in Japan since ancient times, is created by microorganisms, so the taste is of a different quality to that synthesised by human technology. It is not human work.

If you put miso or pickles in an earthenware pot, you create an ecosystem that co-exists with the microorganisms, a kind of world in miniature. Natural products like miso and pickles are a perfect match for the nature 'inside' human beings – that is, our digestive systems – and human beings trying to live in harmony with nature.

When we look at a natural landscape, we see its beauty: however many times we look at it, we will not get bored. We might even be inspired by the dynamic changes that take place within it. Nature (man) blends in well with nature (landscape), and this makes us feel good. We have nurtured life, guided by this good feeling.

The food traditions that form part of a particular culture, which, in turn, has been nurtured by a particular climate, are an example of this. They are not something that have been made over one or two hundred years. They have been honed by experience and accumulated little by little over a thousand years – no – over a period as long as human history.

Some think that the first people who ate *nameko* mushrooms, octopus and other things that are edible despite their off-putting appearance must have been very brave. While this may be true, it is hard to believe that our food culture was created by early humans putting everything they found into their mouths and the repeated failures that inevitably followed. Just like other creatures, I think people probably had some idea of what was nutritious and could be absorbed by the body before they ate it. If nothing else, they must have had skills that we in the modern age cannot even imagine. One such skill would have been food preparation, including complex processes such as removing bitter tastes, which they carried out without anyone having taught them. In order to survive, early humans must have had the ability to sense what they could and could not eat. Then, over a long period of time, the number of foods in their diet gradually increased. Just as the ability of microorganisms to adapt to their environment results in beautiful patterns in nature, small systems were gradually built up and the splendid food culture of each part of the world was created.

One of the things that grew out of these early human skills was the wisdom of different cultures as they adapted to their different climates. Accordingly, when you pick up raw ingredients and use them in cooking, although you may be unaware of it, what you are doing is directly connected to the natural world that forms the background to these cultural developments. I think Japanese people continue to feel a particular sensitivity to nature that results from the unique natural conditions that exist in their part of the world. Compared to parts of Europe and some other Asian countries, the climate and the movements in the Earth's crust beneath Japan are quite extraordinary. In addition to the changes in the seasons, Japanese people have to adapt to small climatic changes on a daily basis, and cope with the complications of nature as a matter of course. Just think about it! Our customs are bound to be different to those found in a climate where the temperature is the same all year round. With respect to food, clothing and shelter, we have been forced to adapt to a climate that is constantly changing, and have refined our skills accordingly.

A Plan for Living

暮らしの寸法

Trusting your body

It is our bodies that receive the rice and miso soup and perceive them to be delicious, but when we eat rice and drink miso soup, I think we feel a comfort that goes beyond that. This might be a sense of security or comfort; it will vary from person to person, but it is something that makes us feel a little bit happy. When I take a mouthful of a fatty piece of meat or tuna, I automatically think 'delicious!', but this pleasure is felt in the part of the brain that is connected to the tip of the tongue. I think there is a difference between the kind of deliciousness that makes the brain happy and the kind that the whole body can enjoy. It is not that the body is insensitive, but it is a sensation of comfort that comes after you have finished eating, a feeling that the body is cleaner . . . as if each individual cell is glad, and this is transmitted to you by the body's sense of well-being. However, the brain often fails to notice this peaceful calm; to me, it's as if the brain were facing in the opposite direction to the body. These days, I think it's a mistake to trust it too much and so I tell myself, 'Don't be cheated by your brain!'

Among the everyday foods that are considered healthy in Japan, rice and miso soup are not particularly exotic, unlike, for example, dried strips of daikon radish or edible seaweed, so they probably do not feature on any gourmet cookery shows. When people eat those types of foods and exclaim in surprise, 'delicious!', I wonder just how genuine it is, because no dried daikon radish can be as delicious as all that. I have heard young people in Japan say that good food 'tastes normal', and I think this is how it should be. Normal 'deliciousness' is the peaceful taste associated with the comfort of daily life. Dried strips of daikon radish just taste normal.

For the person cooking, being told 'it's delicious!' is probably welcome, but that expression can mean different things. Tastes that belong in the home might be described as peaceful and subdued. Mothers often complain that their families do not appreciate their cooking, but if there is no comment, it just means they have established delicious food as the norm. I think it is a sign that those who are eating feel no discomfort and are at peace.

The things we eat everyday taste normal to us. This gives us a sense of security.

If we look at it this way, it becomes clear that we do not eat things just because they are delicious. We hear and see the enthusiastic cries of 'delicious!' and 'tasty!' on TV, in magazines and in social media, but these 'delicious things' that we keep hearing about include many that we can manage without and plenty that I have my doubts about. Fads like these are short-lived and ever-changing. It is important to distinguish between foods that are made to sound delicious and those that actually are. Once you have understood that these are quite different things, then you can decide what to eat.

Rice, Miso Soup, Pickles

Someone once said, 'You can't fight on an empty stomach,' and it is true: when you run out of energy, the body stops moving. People cook to create life and eat to feel well. Sometimes you see people patiently sipping some bitter green juice, probably for its health benefits rather than its taste. When people eat, they are after more than good taste. If something is good for you, your body can sense it at some subconscious level, and the good feeling this creates slowly sends a message to the brain.

Foods that the body craves, like rice, miso soup and pickles, sometimes turn out tasting less than perfect, depending on the circumstances of the creator. Sometimes they will be delicious, sometimes not. Try to think of it like this: there is no need to pay too much attention to the taste, rejoicing over every success and grieving over every failure. This is not because it does not matter, but because you will experience both, and you need to be able to tell the difference yourself.

World-class baseball players like Ichirō Suzuki (who retired in 2019) do not let their happiness depend on whether they hit a ball or not. They need to remain calm and composed at all times, so that they can be ready to hit the next ball when it comes. I think Ichirō improved his everyday performance by focusing on the overall quality of his play. By doing so, he

Trusting your body

managed to improve his successful hit ratio and his intuitive ability to use good opportunities. There is a saying that 'a modest life is the preparation for greatness'. Next time you need to focus on your work, try eating rice, miso soup and pickles. I am sure you will make great progress.

Doing simple things with care

When you decide to cook one soup and one side dish, the stress associated with meal preparation falls away. This alone should ease the mental load, but in addition, you create extra free time to relax. This brings its own joy, as well as mental space. This book was not a result of trying to make household chores easier: one soup and one side dish is not a way of cutting corners. Feeling as though I have omitted certain crucial steps is probably the feeling I hate the most. It is very important to be comfortable with one's own feelings, and so I would like you, dear reader, to understand the thinking behind one soup and one side dish.

I often hear people say that cooking takes a bit of extra effort, but although effort is always praiseworthy, it does not necessarily produce delicious food. I think the misunderstanding comes about because, in

Doing simple things with care

general, making an effort is associated with putting your heart into something or doing something with care. However, with everyday cooking, there is no need to make such a special effort. Home cooking is not something to take great pains over. That is what makes it delicious. (Japanese cuisine has two sides: it is both 'something you have to work at' and 'something you do not have to work at', but I will explain this later.)

The best way to make the most of your ingredients is to cook them simply. However, as I have just said, these days there seems to be a widely held belief that some effort must be involved, that this is what makes it 'cooking'. When I look at Japanese social media, I often see pictures of a soup and two side dishes set out nicely on a tray, accompanied by words like 'slumming it today'. Perhaps whoever posted this is saying, 'Japanese cuisine is easy, normally I make a bit more effort than this.' But this trend of looking down on cooking that is simple and does not require much effort only raises the bar for the one doing the cooking and does them no favours in the long run.

Busy people who succumb to this pressure will think they can just take processed foods and mix them with other ingredients, add a topping, and somehow achieve the desired result just by making it complicated, but this only promotes the misconception that cooking properly involves a big effort. Personally, I tend to think of *this* type of cooking as lazy.

The idea of combining different ingredients to produce a new flavour, or producing a good flavour by layering tastes using different spices and seasonings, is not a typically Japanese approach. It is a Western one. In today's Japan, scraps of different thoughts and philosophies have slipped into and made themselves at home in our lives. Japan's former national football team manager, Alberto Zaccheroni, once appeared on the radio following his retirement, together with an interpreter whom he had known for a long time. He said that he had first tasted *wasabi* in Japan and had become very fond of it. He said he liked the spicy one that came in a tube. The conversation became very animated, and then the presenter said something like, 'That annoying fresh wasabi is no good. It's got to be a tube, right?' as if pandering to his opinion. Now, I don't mean to criticise someone for labelling the real thing as 'annoying' and contributing to cultural erosion ... but I think this type of throwaway remark can have a bad influence on a large number of people.

By holding firmly onto basic criteria and ideas, you will learn to make the right judgements. Japanese

Doing simple things with care

cuisine developed against a background of nature; for Western cuisine, it was human philosophy. The two styles of cuisine produce completely different people. If you are Japanese, you will speak Japanese, and it would be normal for you to cook food in a Japanese way – this is logical. However, in the present day, it would be nice if we could enjoy both Japanese and foreign food culture, having understood the background to each.

I am not rejecting change, but food cultures are not built on dishes thrown together on a whim. In the same way that Japanese cuisine seems to be an endangered species, Japanese home cooking also seems to be dying out. Japanese food culture helps to create the Japanese 'spirit', and this becomes our identity, giving us confidence and trust. Culture is something that should be valued, so we should be cautious when it comes to change. Even if sushi and *kaiseki* (a sophisticated Japanese cuisine served in courses) survive as examples of Japanese cuisine, a food culture from which home cooking has been lost is barely worth having. Home cooking is what gives people strength.

But to return to what I was saying earlier, about cooking requiring effort. I would not refer to the preliminaries, the basics of food preparation, as effort. One cannot chew on a fresh daikon radish if it is raw or without first rinsing off the earth, so one washes it, cuts it into bite-sized pieces and applies heat to it. The different stages of this process are not effort, they are just basic food preparation.

The truth is that home cooking, everyday cooking, was never meant to be any more work than this. Making any more effort is unnecessary, and if you handle the raw ingredients more than you need to, you will inevitably damage them and decrease their freshness. By trying to make them look nicer and deliberately increasing the trouble you take, you will actually make them taste less good, so the effort is misplaced. In everyday cooking, you should not try to change the raw ingredients, instead just appreciate them as they are.

A balance between extravagance and restraint

In Japan, there are two twin concepts: things that are *haré* or ceremonial and things that are *ke* or commonplace. Haré is a special state of affairs, a festival. Ke (which rhymes with 'fed') is the ordinary, the everyday. Everyday home cooking is ke. In contrast to ke dishes, which do not require any effort, we have haré dishes for special occasions. Originally, the distinction was between food made for humans and food made for the gods. The thinking behind them and the way in which they are prepared is therefore the opposite.

On a festive, ceremonial occasion, we pray to the gods, make requests and give thanks. In order to give thanks for and accept the blessings of nature from the gods, we make food for the gods to eat. This is not like everyday food, where one simply tries to make the most of the ingredients; instead, people try to come up with their best ideas and spare neither time nor effort in making them colourful and beautiful. After they have offered this food to the gods, they eat it together with their families and enjoy the rest of the day. There is a special expression for eating with the gods, *shinjin kyōshoku* (literally, 'gods and people eating together').

With ceremonial food it is considered proper to take time, to take trouble, and to think of your entreaties (what you will pray for) as you prepare the food. For ceremonial food, there is no question of cutting corners or saving time, so there is no such thing as 'instant *osechi*' (special dishes that are cooked in advance and eaten to celebrate the New Year). This might be something you decide to eat on New Year's Day, but it will not provide solace for the Japanese heart.

The 'scattered sushi' or *barazushi* (vinegared rice with special things scattered on it, also known as *chirashizushi*) that we eat on festival days is made by layering and combining many different ingredients and then flavouring them with generous amounts of broth and seasoning. It is piled up on decorative serving dishes set aside for that day and served with sake. I remarked earlier on that in Japanese cooking, if you interfere with food you can spoil the flavour,

A balance between extravagance and restraint

but this does not mean the labour-intensive food we eat on ceremonial days is unpalatable: it is exceptionally delicious. The reason for this is that, with ceremonial food that has been developed over the course of history, even though a lot of time and trouble go into making it, and even though it combines various different ingredients, it is carefully designed so that none of the flavours are spoilt. In some ways, the methods follow modern rules of hygiene. Alcohol and salt are used, the broth is drained, everything is cooked separately, and it is all cooled quickly: this is the wisdom of *washoku*, Japanese cuisine. In our food customs we make a clear distinction between one task and another, so that it is possible to eat sashimi safely even in mountainous regions that are far from the sea.

In summary, there are at least two different value systems in Japan: one where effort is made, and one where effort is avoided. If we put these two seemingly contradictory systems side by side, making a clear distinction between the two, and separating them according to the occasion, they each have their own logic. However, in today's Japan, the two have become completely confused. This has been noted by many writers, including by the calligrapher and scholar Kyūyō Ishikawa in *Nijūgengokokka Nihon* ('Dual

Language Nation Japan', Nihon Hōsō Shuppan Kyōkai, 2011), and I feel that the same is true for Japanese food culture. Many people bring the ceremonial value system to their kitchen table and, mistakenly assuming that cooking must involve the labour-intensive dishes demonstrated on cooking shows, suffer over their daily menu.

Traditionally, ordinary people took pleasure in laboriously assembled feasts because they were attracted to expensive things. In Japan, where we attach importance to our appearance in the eyes of others, most hope to obtain at least the same as what others have. Sometimes this results in a desire for things that are beyond one's means, and this can appear at the wrong place and at the wrong time, resulting in a confusion between the ceremonial and the commonplace. In some respects, our present-day lifestyle is so unbalanced, it is as if the feudal lords and the common people were suddenly living together. We long for an extravagant lifestyle, believing that expensive things are inherently better, and hating the things that we need to do as a matter of course. This is where contradictions and impossibilities arise.

According to regional stereotypes, people from Osaka are supposed to be stingy, but in times gone by, gentlemen from that part of Japan would have been

A balance between extravagance and restraint

extravagant idlers. The *kouta* (a Japanese ballad accompanied on the shamisen), the tea ceremony and serving food that was ruinously expensive all created opportunities to exchange trading information. By collecting expensive items and enjoying every possible luxury, indulging their natural sense of fun and sociability, the merchants were able to elevate themselves in the eyes of their clientele and competition. However, as far as these gentlemen were concerned, it was bad form to enjoy this level of luxury on a daily basis, so this is where they tried to scrimp and save. Although they were sometimes considered vulgar, they were able to laugh at themselves. In a sense, they achieved a balance between extravagance and restraint. During their heyday, their skilful way of handling the ceremonial and the everyday were truly admirable. They came across and had an eye for good things, and in their own way, they contributed to Japanese culture. I believe that our happiness is to be found in this equilibrium between a down-to-earth, modest lifestyle and one of luxury.

A modest life is an important preparation

A person's 'daily life' consists of the activities they engage in to live, and this includes their work outside the home. Doing chores inside the home is simply 'living'. In times gone by, I think little distinction was drawn between jobs people did outside and inside the home – they were dealt with in the same way and were connected – but today more importance is attached to work outside the home, and 'living' has become neglected. But I believe that happiness is something found within the home, within our ordinary day-to-day lives.

We tend to live our daily lives with indifference. By definition, they involve repeating the same things every day. But it is precisely because we do this that there is so much to notice. This noticing, in turn, can be a source of pleasure. If you tidy the garden every

A modest life is an important preparation

day, you are probably aware of many things that only a person tidying the garden knows. Even a single stone can become as familiar as a friend. You will know whether it has always been there, or whether it slipped into the garden from outside at some point. A plant you do not know may flower. When spring comes, the buds on the trees in the garden will swell. The green of the leaves will become brighter each day and you will be acutely aware of the changing of the seasons. The weeds will also grow, and you might find your favourite among them.

If you squat down and carefully tidy around the roots of the trees, sweeping up every single leaf, and then water everything thoroughly so that the trees stand out conspicuously against the dark earth, it can be breathtakingly beautiful: as if your very soul feels refreshed. You feel as if the plants are happy. For me, although I am the one looking after the plants, I also have the feeling that they are looking after me. This is all to do with noticing the small signs that appear before something significant happens. People used to say, 'Inattention is the greatest enemy,' and this is probably a good motto.

Sometimes a tree will drop its leaves again as soon as you have finished tidying up around it, just like in a children's cartoon, and you will have a sense of déjà vu: it is as if the leaves of a new tree have fallen in a garden that has just been swept. A new garden is appearing there.

A garden that you see for the first time is beautiful. The fact that it is constantly in flux is beautiful. Flowing water does not decay. This feels good to us because it represents unstoppable time, which is an aspect of nature. Just as the Ise Shrine (one of the most important Shinto sites, located in Mie Prefecture) is rebuilt every 20 years, renewal is connected to eternity. If we focus on the effect of renewal, then work outside the home must be constantly renewed too. If that work becomes a bit too easy, then I think one has to prioritise change, since even a small change can make things fresh again. If one experiences a temporary setback, one can recover; greater competence is accumulated through repetition.

This is a little like having one soup and one side dish for every meal, every day. Even if you set out to make the same thing, it will naturally change with the changing of the seasons.

The Japanese climate is generally warm with frequent rain: rainwater is stored in the beech-covered hills, mineral-rich water gathers in rice fields, and this gradually flows out to create fertile ground, which bears fruit with the changing seasons. This long island country includes every kind of climatic zone, from sub-arctic in the north to sub-tropical in the south, as well as a complex geography with high mountains and low valleys formed by continual changes in the Earth's crust, and as a result, different ingredients and different food cultures have developed in its different regions. These days, wherever you go in Japan, whatever the season, vegetables of a uniform shape are distributed from the same prefecture, but local produce is always preferable. Local fruit and vegetables harvested in small quantities are not distributed commercially because it is not efficient and because they are irregular, and so they are not found at large markets. Instead, they are sold at local morning markets, retailers or other small markets where they can be delivered by small trucks. They are fresh, use few agricultural chemicals and are generally very healthy; consequently, they also taste good. Even just trying to eat locally produced food can change our lives, and it is often enjoyable too.

Everyday Food

毎日の食事

The significance of cooking

There are many people who like to cook properly every day. I am one of them. Maybe this is because somewhere in our minds we sense how important it is to eat; we know it at some subconscious level.

We normally refer to having a meal as simply 'eating' but 'eating' is just one part of having a meal; there is much more to it than this. Before you eat, a member of your family will need to go shopping (in real life or online) and prepare the ingredients. They will wash the vegetables and get everything ready; cook the rice, steam the vegetables, grill the fish and dish it up. Then they will arrange all the plates on the table.

When it comes to the eating itself, there are inevitably certain other actions that accompany it. We tend to refer to all the acts that we do for the sake of eating as 'eating'. We need to move our bodies, stand up, use our hands, use our muscles, and eat in order to live. But the many activities that surround eating, which is the starting point for life, actually also include many of the learning functions required to support intelligence and develop essential skills. Together, they provide us with the capacity to live. I think my body knows these things instinctively, and that is why I want to cook properly every day.

The meal cycle

Go shopping → Get ingredients ready → Cook ingredients → Dish up → Eat meal → Tidy up → (Go shopping)

The significance of cooking

When you have finished eating, you tidy up and put everything away. You take a breath before getting back to the other jobs you had to finish, and then preparations for the next meal begin. Once again, you cook, eat, tidy up. When you get up the following morning, you make breakfast, eat. This daily repetition is what makes up our lives, and before long, its significance takes many beautiful forms; I believe they manifest themselves in each of us.

As human beings, cooking is something we must do in order to survive. However, in the modern world, we can get by without having to cook. This is because we can easily replace cooking and eating with buying and eating food that has already been prepared. But when this happens, people end up discarding the actions (or work) that had been essential for eating. If the interrelation between 'action (work)' and 'eating' disappears, the learning functions acquired in order to stay alive are lost: if you consider how doing certain things in order to eat also nurtures the mind, then it is inevitable that emotional development and balance will be affected in some significant way.

At the same time, in modern society, even if you want to cook, you may not have time, and even if you are working, you may not be able to afford whatever you want. I suspect the problem lies with our social system. Some may call it an inevitable outcome of the principles of capitalist competition, but Kiyoshi Oka, a twentieth-century mathematician who wrote numerous works on Japanese thought and culture, referred to it as the 'struggle for existence'. At the most basic level, this means killing each other in order to survive, but human effort should surely be focused on happiness, not merely survival.

For previous generations, before there were enough resources for everyone, to 'struggle for existence' may have been the right approach, but I wonder how things will be going forward. Just because something is good for the very rich, who only make up a handful of the population, it might not be right for the majority. I wonder how it will be for our children's generation.

I do not really think that we can solve such huge problems with the tiny things that make up our daily lives. I am also not arguing that just because cooking is the right thing to do, you have to cook under any circumstances. But I am trying to make sense of the fundamental meaning of food, because it is what creates life for every single one of us. I also believe that doing the bare minimum can lead to the happiness of every individual.

The significance of cooking

At the very least, I think it is important for people to engage with good, homemade food during the important periods of their lives. I think food is particularly important when you are starting a family, and until your child has become an adult. And, if you want to take good care of yourself, then it is important to live carefully. I want you to cook properly even if you live alone. By doing so, you can keep yourself in check from time to time, 'admonish yourself', to borrow a Buddhist concept, and the order created by good habits will surely follow.

You will need to stand firm! A life without cooking may resemble the 'struggle for existence' that Kiyoshi Oka calls 'nothing but *avidyā*,' a Sanskrit word meaning 'spiritual ignorance' or 'blindness to the ultimate truth'. In Buddhism, this term refers to the ugly and frightening side of humanity.

The peace of mind that the kitchen creates

Juichi Yamagiwa, anthropologist and former President of Kyoto University, is a gorilla researcher. In 2012, I visited his research laboratory at Kyoto University to hear what he had to say about gorillas. According to Professor Yamagiwa, by observing the behaviour of gorillas, some of our closest relatives among the ape family, one can gain insights into what it means to be human. There are things that gorillas do that humans do too; there are also things that gorillas do, that humans don't. In studying gorillas, one is effectively studying humans. This approach led him to write about the differences between gorillas and humans in 'Human Evolution as Seen from the Perspective of Primatology' and 'Humans Seen Through Bionomics'.*

---

* From 'Exploring the Human Mind and Its Social Origin' (Institute for Advanced International Studies) by Juichi Yamagiwa

The peace of mind that the kitchen creates

In these he divides up human life from birth to old age into the following stages: infancy, childhood, the juvenile period, adolescence, adulthood and old age. 'Infancy' is the period when the baby is still breastfeeding. 'Childhood' is when they eat different food to the adults. The 'juvenile period' is that period when they can eat the same foods as adults, but do not participate in breeding. In 'adolescence', they have the capacity to participate in breeding but do not do so. In 'adulthood', they do participate in breeding. He refers to 'old age' as the period when a person has withdrawn from breeding. Among these, there are two periods that do not feature in the life of a gorilla: 'childhood' and 'adolescence'. A gorilla is already quite independent by these stages, but a human is not, being still supported by its parents.

This difference may be viewed in different ways, but rather than thinking of human development as being slower than that of a gorilla, I prefer to think that more time is required for a person to fully grow and learn everything they need to know in order to function independently within human society, which is complex and highly developed. In earlier times, a male child would have had to learn his father's hunting techniques in order to survive; a female child would have had to learn everything that her mother did. During this period, by eating good food, a child would have developed a healthy body and absorbed a good deal of wisdom.

From birth until they become young adults, human children tend to entrust all their meals to their parents, since there are many other things that they must learn. However, even children who do not cook but only eat experience and learn many things unconsciously, through their food.

In my own house, where my place of work and my home are one and the same, there is often food that has been prepared in the course of my work, for example for photo shoots. However, when the photographs are finished, I let those who have been working share the food, or give it to guests to take home, since it is food prepared for work. My wife never once put that kind of treat to one side to feed to our daughter when she came home. I always thought, we are so busy, there is no need to prepare other food especially for her, let her eat what we already have. But my wife would wait for our daughter to come home, and as soon as she heard her shout 'I'm home!' she would start cooking.

The special food that I prepare in the course of my work, and the food that my wife prepares on the spot, are they the same, or are they different? Naturally,

The peace of mind that the kitchen creates

they are completely different. Not because one is fancy and the other is simple, or because of the way that they are flavoured. My daughter probably heard the sound of my wife preparing food for her while she changed out of her school uniform. She could probably smell it too. She probably sensed that her mother was in the kitchen, cooking. Cooking is truly an expression of love. How relieved she must have been to come home! How reassured! She must have felt loved with her whole being. For a child, a parent's cooking is something special. I did not understand the meaning of what my wife did at the time. But I am grateful to her now.

The relief of the kitchen is an unshakeable peace, deep in your soul. A child who has had their meals cooked for them acquires a sense of peace and stability that exists in the centre of their being. Even in the midst of great events, I think it reduces their fear when all they want to do is flee. This peace of mind gives them the composure required to respond to events calmly without becoming flustered. It is also connected to motivation, and the courage needed to set off on a journey into the unknown. When I consider my own experience, this peace of mind comes back as a memory, something profoundly healing.

To eat well is to live well

Dr Ichirō Akizuki (a doctor who survived the atomic bombing of Nagasaki and went on to collect and publish eyewitness accounts of the event) said that our constitution is formed by what we eat, in other words, our constitution and what we eat are inseparable.* For a person to be healthy, their environment is important, and while we may think of the environment as being composed of sunlight, air or water, according to Dr Akizuki, food is the representative element. Through food we can become ill and it is easy to develop health problems due to our eating habits. Conversely, we can be healthy because of what we eat and develop a robust and healthy constitution that means we seldom get ill.

---

* From 'Constitution and Food: the Path to Health' (Clear Publishing) by Ichirō Akizuki (1916–2005, former director of the St Francis Hospital, Nagasaki)

To eat well is to live well

We can also improve our constitution through the things we eat. A person's cells are constantly being renewed, so that within a few months parts of the body are completely regenerated. For this reason, we should eat a good diet consistently and continuously.

Let's talk a little bit more about cooking.

There are certain foods like miso that have nurtured human life by means of traditional technology, and then there is modern processed food: surely everyone knows by now that not all of the latter nurtures life in a healthy way. This is true not only for processed food. From a scientific perspective, there is no food that is perfectly safe and secure. And yet, by preparing it yourself, you can make food safer. Even if you start with convenient processed food, by cooking it yourself you can protect yourself and your family to a certain extent, and so take responsibility for your food.

Food culture originally grew out of the logical methods used for eating things safely in a particular climate. Recently, I hear the word 'convenient' used in place of 'logical', but they do not mean the same thing. When it comes to food, convenience is often achieved by sacrificing the good flavour of the ingredients themselves, as well as the health value of that food.

If you cook yourself, you can decide which foods and which seasonings to use. When you consider

Rice, Miso Soup, Pickles

which ingredients to use, your thoughts might well fly out of the kitchen as you think about wider society and the natural world. If you consider where you will buy your ingredients and from whom, which region they have been grown in and which sea they have been caught in, then you will realise that food connects you to many people as well as to nature. By looking at and touching the food we cook, we can make a direct connection with these fundamental things.

Things that we do not understand with our heads, we can sometimes feel through the act of touching. The mind sometimes gets in the way of what we feel with our bodies, but even things we think of as meaningless can, individually, be valuable experiences. There is no such thing as a wasted experience. I think that by coming into direct contact with other living things, people can develop what mathematician Kiyoshi Oka refers to as our emotions or feelings. This includes things that make our life richer, such as imagination, sensitivity and intuition, and learning how the mind works, which is hard to explain scientifically. One might even say we acquire an awareness of how the body works.

The experience of a child eating food prepared by a parent. The experience of sharing food that you have prepared as a family. The experience of eating food

To eat well is to live well

that you have prepared by yourself. I believe that the relationship between the act of cooking and the act of eating is this: the person cooking transmits all of their experience *as well as* the natural order, which is infinite, to the person eating, and in doing so, connects with them.

As long as we are alive, we cannot escape from the need to eat. This act of 'eating' that we can never distance ourselves from and will always be connected to is directly related to our attitude to life. It is both the foundation for, and the background to, our lives, and reveals who we truly are. It is for this reason that people say, 'To eat is to live,' and that without a doubt, 'To eat well is to live well.' (The French politician Jean Anthelme Brillat-Savarin, who wrote *Physiologie du Goût* ('The Physiology of Taste'), is famous for having said, 'Tell me what you eat and I will tell you what you are,' and, of course, what he means is that the food reveals the man.)

These days we are surrounded by food and we don't have to worry about eating if we choose not to. When it is too much trouble, we can decide not to eat, and we can live without paying much attention to whether the things we eat are good or bad. There is nothing wrong with not thinking about it, and it won't inconvenience anyone else either. Eating what you please, although it might upset the laws of nature slightly, is perfectly acceptable according to the rules made by humans.

But I think eating might actually be something really important. In fact, I imagine most people have already established this with their own bodies. And yet, in the same way that we become absorbed in the minutiae of life that demand our attention, turning our backs on the more important things, like the environment or our children's future, we tend to worry about unimportant matters and postpone the important ones.

However much one might worry about global crises such as the environment, solving them is beyond the capacity of a single person. It is tempting to give up, thinking one cannot do anything alone, and to avoid the issue by distracting oneself with immediate pleasures. I suppose that's just human nature. However, if you were to ask me what you can do with respect to larger problems, I would say, 'Start by eating well.' When someone once asked her, 'What can I do towards world peace?' Saint Mother Teresa apparently answered, 'First of all, go home and love your family.' So please, start by taking care of your own diet.

Whatever you try to do to solve the larger problems, almost everything will require supporters and collaborators. But the good thing about my suggestion that one soup and one side dish is enough is that you can do it by yourself, without first having to recruit your friends. In fact, there are plenty of things to enjoy beyond eating. The achievements of man, who has been a part of nature for 2 million years, are beyond doubt. Place your trust in our cumulative experience and our limitless wisdom.

A Soup and a Side Dish in Practice

一汁一菜の実践

Rice and miso soup with lots of ingredients

With just these, you can get all the nutrition you need every day. If you have a model for your basic meal, it will bring order to your life. In this chapter, I will talk about the method and thinking behind the practice.

The 'one soup and one side dish' meal model

'One soup and one side dish' refers to the meal model that has *gohan* (rice) as the main component, accompanied by *misoshiru* (miso soup) and a single *okazu* (side dish). Traditionally, ordinary families would often not have had any side dish at all, so the model of one soup and one side dish would actually have meant just miso soup, rice and *tsukemono* (pickles).

I know these days many people worry about what they are going to cook every day, but if you think of a soup and a side dish as your basic model, then there is nothing to it. One soup and one side dish is an optimal diet that we can put into practice today. There is no need to go to great lengths thinking about the side dish: if you prepare rice and miso soup, and put a lot of ingredients in the soup, then this can be your side dish too. You can add fish, tofu, vegetables, seaweed and

Rice, Miso Soup, Pickles

other things to the soup, depending on the occasion, and then flavour it using the fermented food product, miso. You could also add a little meat. For your ingredients, choose foods containing protein and fat to build healthy bones, and vitamins and minerals (calcium, etc.) to regulate the functions of the body.

Rice is the source of energy (carbohydrate) that will keep your body and brain working. Traditionally, this would have been enriched brown or white rice (rice cooked with sweet potatoes and *daikon* radishes for bulk). 'Flavour' is provided by pickles. Like miso, pickles are a fermented food product, and in Japan they usually consist of vegetables or fruits pickled with brine and fermented rice bran, but this is really just something salty to go with the rice, and not essential. If you don't have any freshly made pickles, then an *umeboshi* (pickled dried plum) or *tsukudani* (preserved food boiled in soy) would also be fine, and if you have neither of these, and since miso is the best accompaniment for rice, you can just put a spoonful of miso on your rice and eat it that way.

In other words, all you basically need is rice and miso soup. Neither of them is artificial: both are made by nature. With these two, you can have a really well-balanced meal.

The Japanese staple food: rice

Rice cultivation was introduced to Japan 3,000 years ago. Since then, society has become more stable, but the fact that rice was a dry good that could be stored was very important at the time. As a means of paying for labour, rice had the same value as money, and the size of the crop produced by a particular piece of land was used to show how fertile it was. Life was not easy in the early days of rice production, but this was a crop that could support many people, and as a result, Japanese culture began to flower. Life at this time would have revolved around rice cultivation.

Rice farming connected people's lives with nature in a beautiful way: it heightened our sensitivity towards nature and become the foundation of Japanese culture. For Japanese people, and indeed any culture that has rice as its staple food, rice is different to, and more important than, other foods. We harvest the rice (*ine*), thresh it and store it as un-hulled rice (*momi*), then hull it to produce unpolished rice (*genmai*), and finally, polish it to produce white rice (*hakumai*). Although it is just one plant, it has many names, probably because all the people who dealt with it called it something different. When we steam white rice and eat it, we call it *gohan*, using the honorific prefix 'go', since we have come to treasure it.

How to prepare delicious steamed rice

Rinsed rice in a sieve (left) and rice that has absorbed water (right).

Wash the rice, discarding any rice bran that floats to the surface of the water, and tip it into a sieve. The polished rice we buy today contains comparatively little rice bran, and this can be removed by submerging it in water, stirring it, then pouring off the water.

The Japanese staple food: rice

Gently stir it around with your fingers, washing it quickly. If you can still feel the texture of the bran on your fingers, keep changing the water until it runs clear. This will get rid of any saprophytic bacteria that might be present, thereby eliminating any bitter flavour and improving the overall taste, as well as making it less likely that the rice will go off after cooking. When all the cloudiness has gone, put the rice in a sieve (1). If you immerse the washed rice in water again, you make it easier for the bacteria to multiply, so place it in a sieve now to let the water drain off. Rice is sold as a dry good, so after you have given it a quick shake, let it sit for 30–40 minutes to allow it to absorb the water on the surface of each grain (it does not need any longer). Grains of rice that have absorbed water to their very centre are white, plump and moist (2). When the rice is ready, each grain will have absorbed water and become swollen, so the overall volume will have increased. Rice that has been washed and is ready for use is known as *araigome*.

This is the traditional way of preparing araigome. Next, you add clean water, set it on the heat and steam or cook it in the usual way. If you are using an electric rice cooker, please use the 'quick steam' setting that has a reduced cooking time. With araigome, it is better to steam it quickly (the instruction manuals for most modern rice cookers explain that their basic setting assumes the araigome process will be omitted, so that you can steam uncooked rice as it is).

When steaming rice that has been rinsed and allowed to stand, you will need to add an equivalent amount of water. The ratio of araigome to water is basically 1:1, but you can add more or less water as desired. This method will enable you to prepare the best steamed rice, with a delicious flavour and a bold, satisfying texture. If you try it, I think you will notice a marked difference.

How to cook rice cleverly in a way that fits around your daily schedule

If you plan to wash the rice and let it stand for 30–40 minutes before cooking and you are making it for breakfast, you will need to get up an hour earlier than usual, which might be quite difficult. Then again, if you leave the rice sitting in the sieve, after about an hour it will dry out, causing the grains to split and break. Once this has happened, it will be impossible to turn it into delicious steamed rice. But there is a

The Japanese staple food: rice

way to make araigome in advance, so that you can cook it straight away at the desired time. Wash the uncooked rice and put it in a sieve, shake off any excess water, transfer it to a plastic bag and then put it in the fridge until you need it. It will not dry out, and the low temperature in the fridge will make it difficult for bacteria to multiply. This is also a good method to use if, for example, you are going camping and plan to cook rice outdoors.

If you are planning to cook rice for breakfast, then you can prepare your araigome the night before, store it in the fridge, and then add water and set it to steam (on the 'quick steam' setting) as soon as you get up. If you decide to have toast, and end up not using it, then you can just save it until the evening. Then, if you come home late and end up not cooking it again, it will still be fine the next morning. However, be aware that the rice will gradually lose its flavour. As time passes, the gloss on the surface of the rice will become dull, and it will tend to become sticky.

Miso soup with lots of ingredients

Miso is a fermented food that Japanese people have been familiar with since ancient times. One soup and one side dish puts miso soup at the centre of the meal. You can relax because as long as you make miso soup, the meal will be fine. With miso soup, I would not say that the stock or any other single aspect is particularly important. If you set out to make a delicious soup, there are any number of ways to do it, but you should start by understanding the basic principles. You can make miso soup simply by dissolving miso paste in hot water. If you were to dissolve salt in hot water, you would not call it salt soup, but if you dissolve miso, you get a dish called miso soup. I wonder why?

In 'Constitution and Food: the Path to Health', Dr Ichirō Akizuki writes, 'Miso soup is the cornerstone of Japanese health.' Miso soup with lots of ingredients will

Miso soup with lots of ingredients

provide you with adequate nutrition to support and nurture your mental and physical health. Since it has a lot of ingredients, it also fulfils the role of a side dish.

For your miso paste, try to find one that is organic, additive-free and needs to be stored in the fridge after opening. You can even use a combination of different miso pastes if you prefer. You can measure the amount of miso required by specifying a certain number of grams per person, although the amount will depend on the volume and type of ingredients added to your soup and how long they take to cook. However, the amazing thing about using miso as a flavouring is that it will be delicious even if you add a little more or a little less. This is because of the nature of miso. If it tastes too salty, just add a little more hot water. If you just let the miso do its job, then measuring everything according to a recipe won't be necessary.

The liquid in this soup is provided by water. For the ingredients, you can use anything at all. For soy, you can use tofu or deep-fried tofu, also known as the 'meat of the field'. Meat, fish, bacon, ham or eggs can provide protein and fat. Green vegetables, mushrooms and seaweed can provide vitamins and fibre for physical well-being. You can combine any of these, but it is better to have less meat and more vegetables. You can even simmer yesterday's fried

◗ Rice, Miso Soup, Pickles

chicken with vegetables and make miso soup out of these. Miso soup made in this way will taste different every time. It is not repetitive, and although it may not taste great every time, sometimes it will turn out to be surprisingly delicious. Over time, you will realise that good or bad taste is not a major issue. You will also notice that, as you are simmering the ingredients, the broth will sometimes reduce, and instead of miso soup you end up with food cooked or stewed in miso. When that happens, you will understand the difference between a soup – *shirumono* – and a stew – *nimono*.

A quick way to make miso soup for one person

As a general rule, it is a good idea to base any quantities on the bowl you are actually going to eat from. Use a generous bowlful of the ingredients that you have chopped and torn, and another bowlful of water. Chop up any ingredients that are going to provide flavour, such as deep-fried tofu, bacon, ham, meat (chicken or pork) and vegetables to a size that will cook quickly. You can probably just tear up cabbage and mushrooms with your hands. You can also add small dried sardines or dried shrimp: these will not only supplement the flavour of the soup, they also add calcium, so I like to include them.

If you put all of these ingredients in a saucepan and turn on the heat, once the water starts to simmer, most of them will soften quickly, so all you need to do is check that they are cooked and then add the miso paste and dissolve it. When you are preparing a miso soup with lots of ingredients, let it simmer for a little longer after adding the miso, to allow the flavours to blend together.

A few points to note

- **Temperature:** with a smooth miso soup containing just a few ingredients, sipping it when it has just reached *niebana* and is still hot is the best way to taste the flavour of the miso. Niebana ('boiling flower') refers to the state of the soup just before it boils, when the ingredients and miso dissolved in the soup seem to be quivering, and it looks as if a flower is opening from the bottom of the pot. It is considered to be the moment at which the soup tastes most delicious. However, once the miso soup has come to the boil, then it is likely to be delicious at any temperature, and there is no need to serve it

Rice, Miso Soup, Pickles

piping hot. The heat is a sensory pleasure, while the flavour is a pleasure for your tastebuds, and these are two different things.

- **Water quantity:** water is the basis of all cooking, not just miso soup. If you put the ingredients in water and heat it up, the umami in the ingredients will dissolve in the water, creating a 'broth'. Accordingly, if you have chosen ingredients with a strong umami flavour (e.g. bacon, meat), then the soup will be delicious even without stock. Instead of stock, you can also add vegetables that have been fried in oil to get the same effect: fry them first, and then add water. This method is particularly effective with cabbage.

- **Soup for two:** when making soup for two people, if you simply double the amount of water it will become too watery due to the evaporation rate. Instead, start with a bowl of water per person and then reduce the amount of water slightly as the number of people increases.

- **Extra cooking time:** if you want to add ingredients that take longer to cook, such as taro (*satoimo*) or potatoes, simmer these first until they are parboiled, then add the other ingredients.

- **Eggs:** If you are planning to add eggs, dissolve the miso and let the soup come to the boil, then carefully crack the eggs into the soup, turn down the heat, and let them cook for 3–4 minutes until the desired consistency has been reached.

Miso soup – when only the taste counts (left) vs when the appearance counts too! (right)

Above, in the left-hand photo is an everyday miso soup that I made and ate myself. You really can add anything. It will never get boring: you can make something different every day. If you're on your own, you can still enjoy it even if it looks a bit odd. It always seems a shame to leave any in the pot, so I just put it all in my bowl. If I've taken care with the essentials and the ingredients, who cares what it looks like?

Rice, Miso Soup, Pickles

I am cooking for my family, or when we have guests, I find myself paying more attention to how my soup looks (see the right-hand photo). I try to make it look a bit nicer than when I'm eating alone. To improve the appearance, I try to think about colour and how to arrange the ingredients, but it can also be effective just to pour in a little more soup so that the ingredients can barely be seen.

ALL ABOUT MISO

- **There are many different kinds of miso,** many of which are traditionally made in particular regions of Japan, although these days miso is made all over the world. Miso paste is made according to ancient methods with carefully selected ingredients that have been allowed to mature. Considering the different kinds of miso by type, according to their core ingredients, the most popular kind is salty **rice miso** (for example, pale-coloured Shinshū miso), which is usually allowed to mature for around 3 months – although there is also 2-year miso that is given more time to mature. **Soybean miso** is mainly made in Aichi and has a longer maturation period of 6 months to 3 years. **Barley miso**, also known as *inaka miso* ('country miso'), is often made in Kyūshū and is matured for 3 months. These are the traditional types of miso, and the regions of Japan that they come from:

- **Shinshū miso** (rice miso): a rice miso made by mixing soybeans, rice *kōji* (cooked rice that has been inoculated with a fermentation culture, *Aspergillus oryzae*) and salt and allowing them to ferment. At first, it is a bright golden yellow (white miso), but the longer it is left to mature, the darker the colour (red miso).
- **Sendai miso** (rice miso): at 6 months to a year, the maturation period is longer than for Shinshū miso. The flavour is salty.
- **Hatchō miso** (soybean miso): made without rice kōji, using only soybeans and salt.
- **Saikyō miso** (rice miso): since it has a short maturation period, it is very pale. Also known as white miso. A large quantity of rice kōji is used, mixed with salt, and then with cooked soybeans. The mixture is left overnight and then heated to stop fermentation. It is matured over 5–20 days. Mainly made in Kyoto and other parts of the Kansai region, but also popular in Kagawa and Hiroshima. Soup made with this

miso is also referred to as 'celebratory miso soup' or 'miso soup for guests'. For everyday miso soup in Kyoto, ordinary red miso or a blend (mixture) of miso pastes is used.

- **Kyūshū miso** (barley miso): light brown-coloured. Made from soybeans, barley kōji and salt, which are mixed together, allowed to ferment and mature. The maturation period ranges from 3 months to 1 year. Common throughout Kyushu and also around the Setouchi region.

- **A variety of flavours:** if you have two or three kinds of miso, you can vary what you make according to your mood on any given day, and you can also use a mixture. If you take red Shinshū miso, which is very popular, as your standard, you will find that in white Saikyō miso (rice miso), the sweetness of the rice kōji (the umami flavour) is stronger but less salty. Meanwhile, Hatchō miso (soybean miso) has a sour and astringent flavour and less sweetness. Barley miso is quite sweet but not as sweet as white miso, and tastes of barley. In winter, by mixing a little white miso into your red miso, you can make a soup that thickens when it warms up and tastes quite delicious. In contrast, during the hotter months, Hatchō miso (soybean miso) is refreshing and tasty. It also works well for *tonjiru* (pork miso soup) and *arajiru* (a soup made with fish bones). Incidentally, there is also a type of black-coloured miso called *akadashimiso* ('red stock miso'), which is sometimes found in miso shops, but this is just a blended miso made from hardened soybean miso mixed with a softer kind to make it easier to use.

- **The power of miso:** because of the high proportion of salt and other environmental conditions, it is very difficult for the bacteria that cause food poisoning and other sicknesses to survive inside miso. Even *E. coli* O157 would die if it were submerged in miso. It may seem surprising but reports of food poisoning in connection with miso are historically extremely rare. The only things that can survive inside miso are things like lactobacilli (useful bacteria), which are beneficial for human health (please see the website of the Miso Promotion Board, https://miso.or.jp/misoonline/wp-content/uploads/2012/09/miso-english-leaflet.pdf).

Rice, Miso Soup, Pickles

A miso soup that you can make straight away

When you are feeling exhausted, you might reach for a salty snack, but as an alternative, you could dissolve some miso in hot water. This is the most basic form of miso soup. It makes you feel comfortable and relieved, almost as if your body knows that miso is good for you. People used to say, 'Miso soup is good for the soul,' and when someone felt unwell, they were given 'miso tea' made by mixing miso into green tea. The type of miso soup drunk most widely in Okinawa, in the very south of Japan, is *kachūyu*. You just put some miso and a handful of *katsuobushi* (simmered, smoked and fermented skipjack tuna flakes) into a bowl, pour hot water on top, and it is ready. I make it using small dried sardines instead of katsuobushi because they are rich in calcium.

I often fancy miso soup when I am away from home. Miso soup can be a good addition to a Japanese *bentō* or lunchbox, and it takes less time than brewing a cup of tea. In the photograph opposite, the small bottle with the black lid is my 'mobile miso' that I always take with me wherever I go. It can be used for soup, eaten as a topping for rice or used instead of salt, so it is very convenient.

Miso soups that you can only enjoy at certain times of year

These are joyful kinds of miso soup that make you aware of the seasons and leave you feeling strangely renewed.

Spring miso soup

Spring-like things are things that bud. Adding parsley, *mitsuba* (Japanese parsley) or new bamboo that has been fried in oil makes for a superior miso soup. Udo soup, made with mountain *udo* (*Aralia cordata*) that has been cut into thick slices and boiled with tinned mackerel is another one of the joys of spring. Snow peas go on sale early in spring, but you can try using garden peas and broad beans too. In late spring, new onions and new potatoes appear: these go very well with bacon.

When spring comes to the vegetable patch, it is spring under the sea too. There is fresh *wakame* seaweed, and even the stem of the wakame plant, which is only available at this time of year. Spring is the season for fresh shellfish. *Asari* clams are available all year round, but miso soup with clams at this time of year is exceptional. Boil them in water until their shells open, and since they are already quite salty, add a little less miso than usual.

Summer miso soup

At the beginning of summer, miso soup made with *junsai* (water shield) is refreshing and lifts the spirit. *Ayu* (sweetfish) that are sold grilled can be boiled in water and make a stylish soup with akadashi miso. Aubergines become bitter if they are cooked for too long, so I normally cut them into thin slices before adding them to soup, but you can prepare a small feast by cutting smaller Japanese aubergines into thick slices, frying them in a little oil and then adding them to miso soup with a little mustard.

Pumpkin cooks very easily, so you can probably cut this quite thickly too; it will be tasty even if it breaks up as it cooks. If it breaks up completely and the soup thickens, you will have made pumpkin soup. You can also take a vegetable like edamame and mash it up before thinning the resulting mixture with miso soup until you have the desired consistency. This is how to make *surinagashijiru*, a traditional washoku soup. You can also use a fried fish such as *aji* (horse mackerel), break up the meat, add sesame paste and mash it together, flavour it with miso, and finally add *kyūrimomi* (cucumber that has been sliced very finely, using a mandolin if you have one, and salted for 10 minutes to draw out the liquid before being washed and drained) and cold water to make a quick and easy cold soup.

If you carefully drain your miso soup into a clean container and store it in the refrigerator, it will keep for a day or so. Cold miso soup is delicious, but you can also reheat it gently.

Autumn miso soup

Satoimo, or Japanese taro, are delicious in miso soup too. Boil them with their skins on in a separate saucepan, then carefully slip off the skins, crush them with a slight twist, add them to the miso soup and warm it through. If you crush them slightly, they will blend well with the soup. Miso soup made with the small stalks and bulbils of mountain yam is also something special.

Mushroom soup is the kind of miso soup I make outdoors when I go mushroom gathering. I usually take a portable camping stove, miso, chicken and some aubergines. I carefully clean any leaf litter off the mushrooms, stuff as many as I can into the saucepan and simmer them in water. I add aubergines since they are meant to act as an antidote to mushroom toxins. You can also make this at home using two or three different types of cultivated mushrooms.

'Potato drop soup' is made by grating firm Japanese yams to make a purée, taking a portion at a time, dropping it into the miso soup and letting it boil for about 30 seconds. It is light and delicious. Alternatively, add enough miso soup to the purée to achieve the desired consistency and make yam purée soup. Incidentally, if you steam rice mixed with rolled barley and top this with yam purée soup, you get '*mugitoro*', a highly nutritious dish often enjoyed in the hot and humid season.

In late autumn when the mornings are starting to feel cold, I like to add a little white miso to my usual soup and warm myself up with the resulting mixture, which is thick and slightly sweet.

Winter miso soup

Winter is for roots. *Gobō* (burdock root), carrot, *renkon* (lotus root), things like that. Roots that do not soften when you cook them are less suitable for miso soup and may need to be cut into long, thin strips. These days I cook gobō and similar vegetables as they are, without doing anything to remove their slightly astringent taste, and I think they taste better like this. Gobō also goes very well with meat, so you could also try adding it to *tonjiru* (a hearty kind of miso soup made with slices of pork belly and a variety of vegetables).

As it gets colder, we tend to crave richer flavours. Things like *kenchinjiru*, a vegetable soup made with tofu fried in sesame oil. Or *kasujiru*, a soup made from the pressed lees left over from sake production, using the umami flavour of salted salmon, which I often make. It can also be nice to add soft sake lees, torn into small pieces, to your regular miso soup.

Miso soup with seafood

Miso soup with clams. For example, Asari clams, common orient clams or basket clams. The season for marine clams is from spring until early summer, or between about March and June, when people go to the

Rice, Miso Soup, Pickles

beach for *shiohigari* (literally, 'low tide gathering') or clamming. In summer or the middle of winter it is probably better to choose clams grown in fresh or brackish water.

Miso soup with clams is very easy to make. Rubbing the shells together, carefully wash the clams and put them in a saucepan, then measure out and add the appropriate amount of water using a soup bowl per person. If you only have a small number of clams, you could add some *kombu* (a type of edible kelp). Set the saucepan over a low heat and wait until all the clams have opened, bring it to the boil and skim off any scum that forms on the surface, then dissolve the miso in the cooking water and the soup is ready. Asari clams and common orient clams that live in seawater already contain salt, so you will need to decrease the amount of miso you use.

Miso soup made with sea bream or Pacific cod is something very special, however, the pre-cooking is important: quickly dip the fish into hot water and then wash it under running water and carefully remove the scales. Then simply simmer it in water and dissolve the miso. Any kind of fish will produce a good broth, but obviously with smaller fish you need to watch out for bones. With horse mackerel or other fish that still contain bones after filleting, simmer them in water, remove the head and backbone, etc., then use the resulting broth to make miso soup.

You can also make extravagant miso soups with shrimp, prawns, lobster or crab. Each kind of seafood produces its own particular flavour and is delicious in its own way.

Miso soup made with stock

If I am preparing an ordinary meal or cooking for myself, making miso soup by simply dissolving miso in hot water is fine, but if I am making it for someone else, then that is not good enough. So I will set out how to make soup with stock, just in case. With this kind of soup, use slightly fewer ingredients so as to let the soup be the star of the show.

If you use stock, your miso soup will have a mellower flavour and will probably be even more delicious. Instead of simmering your ingredients in water, simmer them in stock. You can use stock made with small, dried sardines, *kombu, katsuobushi* (dried and shaved flakes of fish, usually tuna or mackerel), chicken stock, bouillon – anything works.

The stock does not have to be strong. The end taste is a balance between the stock and the miso, so if you

Rice, Miso Soup, Pickles

want to make a really tasty soup, then you need to be aware of the thickness and type of stock you use as well as its relationship to the other ingredients.

For example, miso soup made from white miso (Saikyō miso) does not go well with a stock that has a strong flavour of fish or katsuobushi. This is because the white miso already contains the gentle flavour of kōji and plenty of umami, so the strong katsuobushi flavour will be very conspicuous. If you are using white miso, just dissolve it in hot water and the soup is ready. If you are going to combine it with a stock, then the gentle umami of kombu might be a good match.

Strong stocks go well with udon (thick noodles made from wheat flour) or sōmen (very thin noodles made from wheat flour) that have been simmered in miso soup. Strong stocks are those made using small, dried sardines or katsuobushi made from mackerel or sardine. They do not combine well with smooth and silky miso soups that only have a few ingredients. With miso soup, miso has the principal role, so stocks that overpower the flavour of the miso are too heavy. You might suddenly decide, 'Today I am going to make some really delicious miso soup!' and make the stock with an extra handful of top-quality katsuobushi. But this will not necessarily make for a tastier soup. It is better to add

Miso soup with lots of ingredients

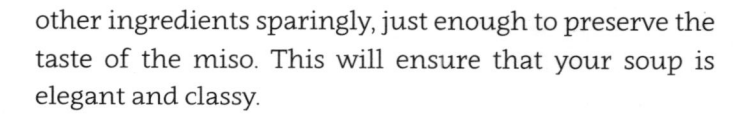

other ingredients sparingly, just enough to preserve the taste of the miso. This will ensure that your soup is elegant and classy.

HOW TO MAKE STOCK

Making stock is often considered difficult, but the only difficult kind is the *suimono* (a delicate, transparent Japanese soup, literally 'something you sip') served in restaurants; other kinds are not hard at all. The stock used for suimono is something special called '*ichiban dashi*' ('first soup stock'). If you are making ordinary stock, choose *niboshi* (small, dried sardines), katsuobushi or kombu. They do not need to be expensive, and you can combine them as desired. To make the stock, put these in water, gently heat them, and when the water comes to the boil, strain it. With niboshi and thicker katsuobushi, it is probably a good idea to soak them in water before putting them on the stove. Simmer on a gentle heat, and by the time the colour comes close to amber, you will have a good stock. You can transfer the stock to a plastic bottle and store it in the fridge where it will keep for 2–3 days.

One soup and one side dish in practice

In this book, I have taken one soup and one side dish as the smallest unit of the meal menu. In Japanese home cooking, rice and miso soup (something with lots of ingredients that doubles as a main dish) will always be the main items. If you use this as the model for your daily meals, I think all of the most important nutrients will be included.

If you add another dish to one soup and one side dish, you will have a soup and two side dishes; add two and it will be a soup and three side dishes. When I do this, I usually reduce the variety of ingredients in my miso soup to maintain the balance. If I have prepared another side dish, I tend to keep the ingredients in my miso soup quite simple, but I might compensate for whatever is missing from my side dish by adding it to my soup. For example, if the side dish is fish, I make miso soup with vegetables. If the side dish is aubergines or pumpkin simmered in soy sauce or something with root vegetables, then I make a miso soup with tofu or deep-fried tofu, or maybe pork and spring onions or green vegetables.

With a miso soup that has only a few ingredients, one can enjoy the light and refreshing taste of the miso soup itself. I will often prepare the broth, add tofu or deep-fried tofu, together with whatever greens are in season, and set it on the heat, dissolve the miso, and as soon as it has boiled, pour it into my bowl. The miso itself provides the flavour, so I think this might actually be the best way to enjoy it. If you like, you can also add fragrant spices such as *sanshō* (Japanese pepper) or *yuzu* (Japanese citron). This type of fragrant garnish for soup is called '*suiguchi*'.

If you add seasonal vegetables when you steam your rice and make *takikomi gohan* ('rice cooked with something mixed into it'), then you can think of this as an additional dish too, and make just a simple miso soup to go with it. Everyday fried rice also contains the ingredients for a separate dish, so combining it with a simple miso soup is fine. In the Kansai region, to the west of Tokyo, they make a dish called *kayaku gohan* that consists of finely chopped shiitake mushrooms, burdock root and other vegetables, cooked in rice with soy sauce. Together with *kasujiru* (a miso soup made with sake lees) containing salted salmon, which is also typical in the Kansai region, this makes for a regular feast. In autumn, rice steamed with chestnuts and a highly flavoured *butajiru* (miso soup with tender pork belly and vegetables) is another wonderful combination. In other words, with a bit of planning and the right combination, you can make a feast out of one soup and one side dish.

If you make miso soup using a tasty stock, and cook the rice with it, then you can also make a delicious miso *zōsui* (a mild and comforting Japanese rice soup or rice porridge, made with vegetables, eggs and meat or fish). When you are making zōsui, if you are going to use cold cooked rice, you can avoid it becoming too sticky by quickly washing the rice in cold water – if you cook it as it is, it will be moderately sticky – but I think it is delicious either way. If you finish it off with grated ginger, then this will give a sharper flavour (in Japanese we call it *aji o todomeru* – 'fixing' the flavour of a dish – when something fragrant is added as a finishing touch). Miso zōsui and pickles can also give you a soup and a side dish.

You can also try adding *suiton* (small flour dumplings) to your miso soup. These are made by mixing a little

One soup and one side dish in practice

hot water into some flour and stirring it briefly. If you mix it too much, it will get sticky and hard, so just mix it briefly and drop spoonfuls of the mixture into the soup. Adding sesame oil will make them taste even nicer. You can also add boiled sōmen noodles or udon noodles. These will give a soup that is slightly thickened and warming, which is comforting and can settle the stomach.

On New Year's Day, it is traditional to eat *mochi* dumplings (rice cakes made from pounded glutinous rice) instead of rice in Japan. In Kyoto or Kagawa, they simmer the mochi in white miso. With *ozōni* (Japanese New Year's soup made with mochi and vegetables) you can have a soup and a side dish at your New Year's meal too. Alternatively, you can make *yudōfu* (hot tofu) by putting some cold water in a saucepan and adding kombu and tofu, and if you put some rice in a hot bowl and add the tofu and its stock, with a spoonful of miso on top, you will have a dish called *uzumitōfu*. The miso will gradually dissolve as you are eating to make miso soup. If you think of miso as a seasoning, you will be able to use it in any number of ways.

One soup and one side dish is a style of eating

You might be asking yourself, if I commit to eating one soup and one side dish, does that mean I can't eat Western food? Do I have to give up bread? What about pasta? By suggesting that we should eat one soup and one side dish, I am not advocating some kind of stoic health regime. Personally, I eat bread too, and I make both Western and Japanese side dishes.

In other words, it is fine for 'one soup and one side dish' to form your basic style (or philosophy) of eating. You can simply bear the basic idea in mind when you decide what to eat. Even if you substitute bread for rice, you can still make a soup and a side dish. Pasta and miso soup is fine too. Miso soup, which is the central pillar of 'one soup and one side dish', is considered to be the mainstay of Japanese health, so I try to have it at least once a day. Even if there are days when

One soup and one side dish is a style of eating

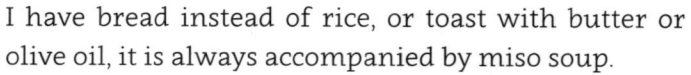

I have bread instead of rice, or toast with butter or olive oil, it is always accompanied by miso soup.

Some people might be surprised to hear me talk about miso soup and bread, but as I get older I feel less bound by rules and expectations around food, and think nothing of putting toast or milk in my miso soup, or even putting milk on my rice. I have actually seen miso soup containing toast in a recipe book that is at least 50 years old.

This may all seem strange because we are constantly told that one must not use butter in washoku, or Italian food must be like this, French food must be like that, and so on.

The way I see it is that we do not need to imitate foreign styles of cooking too religiously or be too purist about our own. I think it is fine to 'eat whatever is there' when you are at home. People who do not cook can do this too. There is no need for the person who normally cooks dinner to get upset if they are going to be late home. They can just tell their partner or whoever is waiting at home, to 'eat something appropriate'. Then the person at home is free to eat what they like and the one running late can simply leave them to it. It's easy for someone on their own. They might fry some bacon they find in the fridge, heat up some miso soup, add some cold rice and the bacon to it, and make bacon-miso-zōsui. That is actually quite delicious, and I think it's fine to have days like these sometimes. It does not mean you have bad eating habits, it is just life, and it is all quite natural.

What I am trying to say is that there is no need to go to the trouble of cooking something special if you do not have the time or the head space. That is not my point at all. Even if you have time, life is busy, and there are bound to be occasions when you don't feel like cooking, or don't feel like cooking very much. If there is not enough for seconds, you can just have extra rice and miso soup. If you decide to eat nothing but rice, miso soup and pickles, and then come across something sweet, you might have that with a cup of tea. You will probably also have some seasonal fruit, and you probably want to try any treats that your visitors have brought. Even if you set out to stop at one soup and *one* side dish, it usually turns into a soup and two or three.

Choosing a soup and a side dish does not mean sacrificing more extravagant meals. You will have different kinds of days, and that is as it should be. You will want to eat meat sometimes, and salads. When you are on holiday, slow down, have a late breakfast, an early supper or cook a feast – I hope you enjoy it! However, when you make a soup and a side dish your basic pattern, and establish order in this area of your

One soup and one side dish is a style of eating

life, various different pleasures will naturally present themselves.

When there is another side dish, I use fewer ingredients for my miso soup. Fried rice counts as rice and a side dish. I try to create menus that strike a balance between the soup and the side dish.

With zōsui (rice porridge), you can create a soup and a side dish in the same bowl. This is the style of eating I call 'one soup and one side dish'.

Those Who Cook and Those Who Eat

作る人と食べる人

In the following section, by looking at the situation from various different perspectives, I would like to consider the state of home cooking in Japan and the future of washoku, that traditional Japanese art of cooking that is so closely bound up with Japanese identity.

In modern Japan, there are foreign restaurants serving food from all over the world. Everyone is very familiar with foreign food and even within the home there are now spices and flavourings that were unknown in Japan until recently, as well as strange, processed foods. People say that Japanese food has become the 'richest cuisine in the world'. But conveying delicious flavours is not the only purpose of food.

What does home cooking set out to deliver? I think it aims to understand the connection between eating and living, and to give every individual warmth in their heart as well as sensitivity. It fosters the power to turn this understanding into another person's happiness, as well as our own.

The aim of 'one soup and one side dish' is to create a more sustainable kind of home cooking, and beyond this, a life to which order has been restored. It aims to create a way of living that can be passed on to future generations, one that returns the meaning of 'family' to the life of every individual. Beyond this, 'one soup and one side dish' is a way to get to know Japanese people as well as Japanese food.

Professional cooking and home cooking – thoughts

For many people, cooking means preparing food while thinking about the person who is going to eat it. While this is no doubt true, it does not mean listening to every single request from the dinner table and responding accordingly. In recent years, the media has tried to demonstrate the attitude, spirit, hard work and effort of elite professional chefs, perhaps in the hope that this would entertain the general public. Many things that were previously kept hidden have become public knowledge, and many people now believe that being a professional chef means something very narrow and specific. At the same time, restaurants have started to extol the virtues of the customer and become more attentive to their needs. Customers, in turn, have responded to this situation by becoming ever more vocal about what they want.

Rice, Miso Soup, Pickles

Now that digital cameras and smart phones have become ubiquitous, and people have started to take photos of restaurant food and post them on social media, some clearly think that because the person who eats is the one paying, they can leave food on their plate, eat in any way they want, and judge that food in any way they like. But this tendency to treat the person eating as superior to the person cooking troubles me.

For restaurants to give in to the unreasonable demands of customers is not the right answer. Good cooking is like carrying a bowl of soup through a busy room filled with customers and service staff. The only proper way to carry it is to hold it level, being careful not to tip it to one side or the other so that the soup does not slop over the edge. Essentially, the relationship between the restaurant and the customer is a relationship of equals, just like that between two ordinary people. Even in a restaurant, considerate people will put themselves in the shoes of the people working there, will behave with good manners and in a way that is appropriate to the setting. When people can do this, I think it is lovely.

The goal of the professional chef is to satisfy the customer using the techniques available in and outside

Professional cooking and home cooking – thoughts

the kitchen, while maximising cost performance. In contrast to the work of the professional, home cooking is not remunerated, and although this does not need repeating, I am stating it again for good measure. The meaning of food prepared by a professional chef and food prepared at home is *completely* different. Home cooking is something simple and plain. Its goal is to nurture your own health and that of your family. Not everything is possible; do not do anything that makes you feel uncomfortable. If it's delicious enough, if it 'tastes normal', then that is fine for now.

Home cooking needs to happen every day. If there is a child in the family, and unless you are away on a trip somewhere, you cannot take a day off and not prepare any food. Giving children food to eat is the adults' duty. Whatever the situation, you need to give your children something to eat. The essence of home cooking is not a game. It is an essential part of life.

The safety and security offered by home cooking, over and above its nutritional value as food, is a given. At home, children can have no doubts around food; they must trust it unconditionally. This gives their parents a certain responsibility, which they discharge using their experiences and through the strength of their affection. And even if they put a huge effort into cooking for their children, there will probably be times when, because they are busy at work or for some other reason, they cannot do as much as they want. There will sometimes be times when, with a heavy heart, they put pre-prepared food on the table alongside things they have made themselves. Children can easily tell whether something has been made by their parents or not. Even if nothing is said, they will not be fooled. But this is because they have already learnt so much, because their parents have worked so hard – this is why they notice. They also know that it is sometimes better not to say anything, and that father and mother are doing their best for them even now.

The most important thing that we can do as people is to *live our lives to the fullest*. I don't think it matters whether you are good or bad at cooking, dexterous or clumsy, skilled or unskilled. The thing that you do with all of your heart is the most genuine, and being genuine is the most beautiful and precious thing of all. I believe this is something that becomes firmly imprinted on the minds of children. If their parents are living life to the fullest, then this is the essence of parental education, and even if there are times when children cannot understand their parents' feelings, their experience will deepen over time, so that when

Professional cooking and home cooking – thoughts

they become adults themselves, they will come to understand. In the words of Hiroshi Shimizu, whom I love and respect, 'Home-cooked food that asks for nothing in return is the work that makes life."

---

* Hiroshi Shimizu, Emeritus Professor of Tokyo University, Director of the NPO, *Ba no Kenkyūjo* (The Laboratory of Place), Doctor of Pharmaceutical Sciences. Specialises in the science of life, bioinformatics and the philosophy of life and place.

Home cooking doesn't have to be delicious

When I was a child, I lived in Osaka. A well-known author lived in the neighbourhood and he became acquainted with my father. One day, my father ran into him when he was going for a walk, and they got talking. The problem was the author's wife. A famous teacher of French cuisine was coming all the way from Tokyo to give lessons, and she had asked the author if she could go. Apparently he answered, 'Yes, as long as you don't try to recreate the recipes you learn at home.' That was surely not the answer she was hoping for. But what he was probably trying to say was, 'I'm content with the food you always cook, I really like it, please carry on making what you've always made.' At the time, it clearly wasn't the done thing to copy food served in restaurants at home, and I think people felt shy about it.

What is 'innovation' in the context of home cooking? It might be cooking the gobō for a bit longer and cutting it up fine so that it's easy for grandpa to eat. Or transferring whatever is left in the serving bowl to a smaller container for a child to eat later. It does not have to mean making separate dishes for each member of the family, but can be the small things that you do. Really small things, whatever you can manage. The person who eats it may not notice that you have gone to any trouble. But I think the knowledge that this food has been made for them will register with them subconsciously.

Personally, I think it's actually more important *not* to be too inventive in home cooking. The reason is, one's family finds peace of mind in the fact that there is little variation and that it barely changes. This is one of the reasons why I cook things that one doesn't get bored of.

If I am having dinner in a place where there are no vegetables on the menu, then I might put a lot of vegetables in my miso soup at lunchtime, although I'm sure I do this subconsciously. When the act of cooking is motivated purely by the desire to nourish ourselves, I think we automatically select healthy things to cook. The person cooking thinks about the person who will be eating. Cooking means there is already love. The person eating is already loved.

Rice, Miso Soup, Pickles

The experience of eating as a family is very important. The question a child is asked most often until they reach adulthood, at least around a Japanese table, is probably '*Oishii?*', 'Does it taste good?' The child learns how to say, 'It's a bit strong,' or 'It tastes a bit different to normal today.' The parent might reply, 'Well done, that's right! Those are the vegetables that granny grew in her allotment.'

The food we have at home is not always fresh. It goes without saying, but sometimes there are things that get overlooked, or leftovers that start to go bad. 'I found these potatoes lying in the bottom of the vegetable drawer, sorry.' 'Don't eat that, it's starting to go bad.' It's not always just a question of 'Does it taste good?' or 'Does it taste bad?' and children learn this too.

When I was a child and lost my appetite because I had caught a cold, my mother used to make me *okayu* (a Japanese rice porridge made with rice and water). As I recovered, she would gradually make the flavour stronger, and when I was almost better, she would steam some flounder for me. Flounder is a white-fleshed fish that is easy to digest; the flesh comes off the bones very readily and it is easy to eat. My brother used to get my mother to debone his before he ate it, but I would always persevere on my own, so my mother would praise me, saying, 'You're so good at eating. You eat fish so nicely.' I was so pleased by this that ever since then I have tried to eat fish nicely.

In food education, we are always taught about the importance of eating together, of sitting down as a family around the table. However, where the family runs a business or where one or both parents are working, this will not usually happen, and the children might heat up food that their parents have prepared and eat it by themselves. I imagine there are many households like this. But they have already been given the most important thing – home-cooked food, that is, love itself. It is not just eating together that is important.

A young person who is home alone because their parents are going to get home late might be quite delighted to find a plate in the kitchen with all the ingredients for something like *nabeyakiudon* (a one-pot noodle soup that is a Japanese winter staple). On the plate are udon, raw chicken, *kamaboko* (a steamed fish cake), shiitake mushrooms and chopped spring onions. They can put it all in an earthenware pot, add some dashi stock and set it on the stove, adding the udon when the stock has come to the boil. The evenings that I spent on my own, eating nabeyakiudon in front of the television, are precious memories for me.

Rice, Miso Soup, Pickles

Home cooking doesn't always have to be a feast, and it doesn't need to taste good all the time. Children have all sorts of experiences at home. Every single one will be useful when they leave home to join society. Whether you do it well, or do it badly, the most important thing is just to put your heart into it.

The relationship between those who cook and those who eat – 'eating out'

Let's think a little more about the relationship between those who cook and those who eat.

There are many different kinds of restaurants, and people who cook have many different goals. Here I would like to imagine one specific restaurant. This restaurant is a business, so if it does not make a profit, it is not viable. However, the chef owner not only aims to make a profit, he also aspires to bring people joy through his cooking, while at the same time developing his own skills. Through his cooking, he would like to make his customers happy, even if just for a short time. He wants to offer dishes where familiar ingredients, such as seasonal vegetables, are cooked with a twist,

Rice, Miso Soup, Pickles

and he also wants to use some exotic, slightly expensive ingredients that his customers would not normally eat at home. It is a French restaurant: it is a given that the food will be delicious. He also wants people to have a special time there, and to want to come again.

I have created a diagram (see opposite) setting out the relationship between the chef owner and the customer – the person who cooks and the person who eats. What kind of information is exchanged between the parties while the various actions take place: the chef owner *giving* (1), the customer *receiving* (2), the customer *giving back* (3) and the chef owner, in return, *receiving* (4)?

What the chef owner is giving (1) is: the origin and meaning of the unusual ingredients; inspiration (ideas); the richness and beauty of the presentation; rich and delicious flavours; a comfortable and tasteful space, which is lit in a relaxing way; an evening to remember.

What the customer receives (2) is: new knowledge to satisfy their curiosity; an unusual dining experience; a feeling of abundance; a sense of well-being.

As for what the customer gives back (3), this includes: gratitude, payment and word-of-mouth recommendations to enhance the restaurant's reputation.

What the chef owner receives (4) includes: a sense of accomplishment and profit.

The relationship between those who cook and those who eat

Exclusive Gourmet Restaurant

Creates:
- Food that will be rated by critics and generate a profit

Must consider:
- Premium and unusual raw ingredients
- What is in season
- Cost

> Person cooking (chef)

0. Reservation details:
- Name
- Budget
- Number of people
- Time and date
- Dietary preferences

1. Chef provides:
- Cooking skills
- Raw ingredients
- Information about cooking
- Creativity
- Heartfelt hospitality
- His personality

2. Customer gets:
- Delicious food
- A special time
- Nice memories
- Enjoyable conversation
- Knowledge about food
- Sense of well-being
- Appreciation

3. Customer gives:
- Payment
- Appreciation
- Recommendation

4. Chef receives:
- Profit
- Satisfaction
- Learning

> Person eating (customer)

Rice, Miso Soup, Pickles

If it is the type of restaurant people go to for the pleasure of eating, then there will be an exchange of experiences and information appropriate to the price; the interaction between the chef and the customer will be well-balanced, smooth and give them both satisfaction; and a relationship of mutual trust will be created.

However, with a chain restaurant, where there is no chef owner, the objectives of the customer will naturally be slightly different too. Depending on their circumstances (the number of people in their party, etc.), what they are looking for (1) might be: a reasonable price, speed, exciting tastes and the satisfaction of a full stomach. The types of cooking that respond to these needs (2) will be things that can be served quickly and that are popular with many people (e.g. hamburgers, pasta, curry, etc.).

The information that is exchanged in this type of situation will naturally be rather scant and shallow, and if the pleasure that the customer receives (3) is the satisfaction of having eaten good food and then some, they will be perfectly satisfied. The customer cannot see the faces of the people who prepare her food, and what the restaurant receives (4) is simply the profit. In this type of situation, the level of information exchanged is relatively low.

The relationship between those who cook and those who eat

Chain Restaurant

Offers:
- Popular staple dishes served at a cheap price
- A space where you can be with your friends

Must consider:
- Information acquisition
- Distribution cost
- Convenient location

> Person serving

1. Customer seeks a venue that is:
- Familiar
- Quick, lively and cheap
- OK with big groups
- Popular

And that:
- Rewards loyalty

2. Restaurant provides:
- A bright space ...
- ... where you can make a noise
- Dishes that are easy to enjoy
- Stimulating flavours

- A variety of choices
- Cheerful service
- Speed

3. Customer gets:
- A fun time
- A full stomach

4. Restaurant gets:
- Profit

5. Customer offers:
- Payment

> Person eating (customer)

▼ Rice, Miso Soup, Pickles

If a meal consists of a ready-made bentō, some *onigiri* rice balls (balls of steamed rice compressed into a triangular or cylindrical shape, often wrapped in *nori* seaweed and prepared with a variety of savoury fillings) or sandwiches that you buy at a convenience store or supermarket, the relationship between the person cooking and the person eating falls away, and there is only the person eating; there is also no exchange of information.

Convenience Store Food
Simple, convenient, cheap

> The person preparing the food is invisible

Store gets:
- Payment

Person eating (customer) gets:
- Excitement of choosing what to eat
- Their hunger sated
- Taste experience?
- Nutritional value?
- Safety?

The relationship between those who cook and those who eat – 'eating at home'

The preparation of home cooking is an act carried out every day in order to nurture your family in body and mind. The person cooking prepares a particular dish on the basis of the experiences and associations that form the background to that dish, while bearing in mind the needs of the family members who will eat it. The person eating, by consuming the meal that has been prepared for them, not only fills their stomach but also takes in whatever the person cooking was thinking of as they cooked, whatever makes up the background to that food. The person who has cooked will hopefully be able to enjoy several things once they have

Rice, Miso Soup, Pickles

finished cooking, such as the atmosphere around the table, and the conversation of their family as they eat the food they have prepared.

Home Cooking
Takes place every day and nurtures life

1. **Background to the cooking that the mother/father provides:**
- Experience/knowledge
- Personality/food culture/customs
- Conditions/season/weather that day
- Budget/raw materials/time
- Cooking skills/techniques/cooking time

> Person cooking (mother/father)

Information from child:
- Are they working/exercising?
- What did they have for lunch?
- What time do they want dinner?
- What do they fancy eating?
- Likes and dislikes?
- How are they feeling?

- Wisdom
- Connection
- Manners (everyday/celebrations)
- Traditional culture (seasonality)
- Health
- Nutritional value

2. Child gets:
- Affection
- Energy for life
- Confidence
- Conversation
- Achievement
- Reassurance/joy
- Memories

3. Child gives:
- Emotion
- Health
- Growth
- Development
- Special words said at the start and end of the meal – 'I humbly receive,' and 'That was a feast.'

The relationship between those who cook and those who eat

- Itadakimasu/gochisōsama deshita
- Sense of well-being
- Love/appreciation
- Filial piety

4. Mother/father gets:
- Sense of well-being
- Information (explicit and implicit)

Person eating (family member/child)

If we now take the person cooking to be the mother and the person eating to be the child, then, in the midst of the various actions that take place here – the mother *giving* (1), the child *receiving* (2), the child *giving back* (3) and the mother, in turn, *receiving* (4) – there is an almost infinite amount of information being exchanged, both consciously and subconsciously (see diagram). This is particularly true where three meals are cooked at home every day.

When the mother gives (1), the background to her cooking consists of what is happening on that particular day (the season, day of the month, day of the week, how much capacity she has, her mood, what ingredients she has available, the time she can dedicate to cooking, her budget, etc.) and the experiences she has accumulated up to that point (her knowledge of the weather, nature and ingredients, her culinary skill, her character, her tastes and preferences, her own customs with respect to food culture). She will prepare the meal considering the circumstances of the person who will be eating (age, sex, food preferences) as well as their condition at that specific time (their behaviour, emotional state, physical health and how their stomach feels on that day).

What the child receives (2) – and indeed consumes in its entirety – will include the mother's affection or emotional state, a sense of satisfaction and nutritional value, together with the mother's particular circumstances and experiences.

The child 'gives back' through their emotional state, and over a longer time-period, their health, growth, development and the lifestyle they embrace.

What the mother ultimately receives in reward, together with all the information transmitted by the child, is the mental state of the child, including their satisfaction after having eaten, and this all creates a sense of well-being.

Over the course of a single meal, whether those involved are aware of it or not, a large amount of information is exchanged, which includes both facts and feelings. This is repeated several times each day, becoming part of the accumulated experience of the person eating. This exchange of information fosters the emotional development of the child.

The relationship between those who cook and those who eat

As a result of all the things that are stored in the body as data, thanks to this exchange of information, I believe that children develop the criteria that enable them to make judgements. An unwavering, unchanging *constant* is created within them. Without experience they will not have this constant. And without this constant, they are unable to compare, and will be unable to judge. With regard to food, having this constant means that when they see a piece of food, they can see it and judge it: can I eat this safely? Does it look tasty or not? If it is good, what will it taste like? Does it taste different to normal, and if so, why? It is not something they need to consider carefully. These are split-second judgements that they make unconsciously: this is instinct.

The value of food is more than its taste or colour: when you select something to eat, you need to grasp the whole character of that food, accurately and in that moment. Of course, I think this 'constant' goes on to become the basis not just for judging food, but for judging people, distinguishing between good and bad, telling the difference between real and fake, and cultivating the imagination. When children grow up, this manifests as their ability to live in modern society, and together with the good memories they have formed, it will probably help them to deal with the many judgements they will be required to make in the future.

We develop our identity and the ability to make people happy through food. This includes the ability to make ourselves happy too.

Discernment

Establishing the criteria required for making judgements also means noticing the difference between what you have experienced before and what you are experiencing for the first time.

The work of a restaurant, or indeed a restaurateur, is to make customers happy. He can anticipate the seasons, and if he can get hold of the first of the season, include it in the menu somewhere, and communicate the changing of the seasons to the customer. Or, when it gets warmer, he can change the way he prepares the yellow *takuan* (a pickled daikon radish with a crunchy texture and a sweet and tangy flavour), cutting it along the grain and reflecting the mood of the new season by bringing out this refreshing texture. Rearranging the dining space to adapt it to the warmer weather, hanging new pictures or doing small repairs or renovations to the building will have the same effect. A customer who notices small changes like these is a joy for the restaurateur. If he receives their praise, he will be happier still; he might say to himself, 'As I thought, that is a good person,' and respect them for it.

Meanwhile, for the customer, the fact that they noticed something by themselves shows insight, and this will give them a sense of satisfaction. I call people who have this sort of insight 'people who take pleasure in things'. When I am working, what makes me happiest is people who take pleasure in what I make. People who take pleasure in what I make are people who understand, and I want to sell good things to people who understand. I think people who take pleasure in things must be aware of what they are doing, and I imagine they are appreciated wherever they go.

Taking pleasure in things means that you can be moved, it means you can be happy. You notice people's love and kindness. It is the capacity to feel love. If you have received plenty of love through the experience of someone cooking for you every day, three times a day, then perhaps this is obvious. If you have received this kind of unconditional love, then you can probably give love to others. This is the relay of love, what Professor Hiroshi Shimizu calls the 'giving cycle'. According to Professor Shimizu, when we do someone a favour, we often want our name to

Discernment

be remembered, we seek recognition and acknowledgement. By contrast, making a true gift involves only the act of giving without seeking any recognition. Doing things for people other than ourselves is part of human nature: the act of giving generates other acts of giving, and the generosity we show others eventually comes back to us. This idea of selfless giving is central to the tea ceremony: the host prioritises the well-being and the needs of their guests in all their actions.

A person judges whether food is good or not with the help of their five senses and their experience, and can also obtain pleasure and different emotions from that food. This is because, as well as appreciating the food with their senses, they evaluate and enjoy the flavours, all the time being aware of the information that provides the background to the food. If someone eats something, knowing nothing about either the person who made the food or its ingredients, with no background information at all, I am not sure whether they will be able to find it delicious – I think they will feel hardly anything.

For foods that someone is already familiar with, especially things they have good associations with, they already have sufficient information. In those situations, they will use their five senses and will eat the food already thinking, before they begin, 'This will be delicious.' Or they might think, 'It seems a little chewy today,' or they might remember the season, and think, 'It's a little too early for this, I wonder how it will be,' and using their own criteria, and the breadth of their experience, they may sometimes feel some doubt.

However, they will not think these things in the order I have written them down. The whole body makes these decisions instantaneously and unconsciously, and as a result, these predictions will be extremely accurate. They are hypotheses, but they are certainties: even if they cannot be explained rationally, they are correct. It means that this person has already established their own definite criteria through their many daily experiences of eating. Then, when this person comes across something splendid that exceeds their own decision-making criteria, they will feel inspired and moved. It will be a pity if they are disappointed, but by questioning the discrepancy between what they expect and what they experience and coming up with an answer, they will develop an even more accurate sensitivity. When knowledge and experience connect, wisdom begins to work. Noticing and discovering things for oneself is a priceless joy.

Discernment

Supposing I have a rice bowl at home. It is something that has had no special value for me up to this point. If I pick it up and look at it, nothing comes to mind. However, if someone whom I respect or someone I trust tells me, 'That is a very fine rice bowl, you know,' then the rice bowl for which I had not felt anything before suddenly becomes precious and attractive. Have you never experienced something like this? It is something that tends to happen when you are still young, but by accumulating this type of experience, you develop the criteria for appreciating things.

If children grow up seeing their parents eating something with pleasure, even if they hate it when they are small, in time they will learn to like it. As far as children are concerned, food is very important: they learn so much from it, develop so many skills, and eventually understand that it is food that gives them the strength to live and to do everything they want to do.

Accordingly, if someone has been properly exposed to this kind of experience as a child, they will probably develop the capacity to make judgements quite naturally. The value of the information that their parents have passed on to them will be very high, and they will be able to make the right decisions, even if they encounter unreliable information or annoyances in the course of their work. This is because they have developed the criteria to judge all sorts of things.

The foundations are important, whatever you do. If you do not master the foundations, you will not be able to do anything. If you entrust food to someone you do not know, you cannot accept their information without question – you must distinguish between good and bad in order to be able to choose your food. You won't necessarily be able to choose good food on the basis of your usual criteria, so you will probably need to investigate the background to that food in order to judge whether it will be good or bad. Good food should not have a harmful effect on the environment, should be beneficial for the producer and the consumer and its production should be cyclical and sustainable, like nature. Good food should cause absolutely no harm to people but instead should nourish life.

In modern society, there seem to be many who accept the authority of reported information without question. There are probably also those who think things like food are unimportant, or do not think too deeply about them. Maybe they think food is so familiar, they cannot be bothered with it, or take any detailed interest in it. But there is a pitfall here. The

Discernment

question of how much interest you ought to take in your own food is something that everyone will answer differently, but by being even slightly aware of what you eat, you will accumulate experiences over time, and it will make a difference in the future, in a variety of ways.

The Origins of Delicious Food

おいしさの原点

Japanese culinary sensibility: think less, feel more

In December 2013, washoku (the traditional food culture of Japan) was added to the UNESCO Lists of Intangible Culture Heritage. The reasons for its selection, against the background of Japan's rich *natural* heritage, included the following:

- It respects the flavours inherent in the raw materials it uses (it celebrates the seasons in which fruits and vegetables are at their best)

- It represents a healthy dietary lifestyle with an excellent nutritional balance (hardly using any animal fats)

- It accompanies the events of daily life (with special dishes for seasonal festivals such as chirashizushi and osechi ryōri)

- It expresses the changes in nature (through its beautiful presentation)

Surely it is obvious that the same applies to Japanese home cooking, which is so deeply connected to the health of the people of Japan and the sentiments of their daily life! Why is it that, despite this, the media are only ever interested in talking to famous chefs? Why do they not go and find the mothers and grandmothers who are keeping Japanese home cooking alive?

Fortunately, there are still a great many people in Japan who show their gratitude for the blessings of nature in the way they live, and who are also good at cooking. Japanese readers, go to your grandmothers and tell them, 'Grandma! Your cooking has been recognised as an Intangible Cultural Heritage! Isn't that amazing? Isn't it great? Congratulations!' Japanese teachers, tell your students that their mothers' and their grandmothers' home cooking has been internationally recognised, that it will now be carefully preserved, and tell them what this means.

Japanese culinary sensibility: think less, feel more

The work that Japanese women do in their homes, which supports so much of the culture of our daily life and which has been passed down through the generations, is generally not recognised by society, and is barely ever praised. I think this is a great shame.

One of the major premises for the listing of washoku as an Intangible Cultural Heritage was the respect that it accords to nature. Japanese cooking typically makes a feature of the fine tastes that are to be found within the changing seasons. It would be a slight exaggeration to say that the only ones who get the best out of every season are the Japanese and the wild birds and animals ... but if you consider the breadth, detail and depth with which seasonality is enjoyed in Japanese cooking, then you will see what I am getting at. This is particularly noticeable in the way in which seasonality is divided into three phases: *hashiri*, *sakari* and *nagori* (very simply put, the harbinger of the new season, the product in season, and the last of the season), and the way in which the beginning and the end of life is felt and perceived with the five senses. The idea behind Japanese cooking that everything should be in line with the seasons makes us aware, through our senses, that our bodies are part of nature.

Rice, Miso Soup, Pickles

Things to do with the emotions appear in quiet places. If you pay close attention to the small changes that occur when you are cooking, you will see that they are evident, hidden in things like sound, colour, fragrance and texture. By following nature in the way you treat ingredients, instead of going against it, you will create a clean taste, free of bitterness. You need to avoid damaging the ingredients – you almost need to sense how it feels to be the food. The evidence that this is the correct approach can be found in the comfort of this clarity, this cleanliness. If you are quiet, you will have many such heart-warming moments while you are cooking, when you think 'Ah, that's nice!' Try to notice these moments and let them guide your cooking!

People say that Japanese food is different to other types of cuisine. I think this might be because with Japanese food, both in the cooking and in the eating, we are not only looking for a good taste. We distinguish between an exciting taste that delights the mind and a good taste that delights every cell of our body, and enjoy them separately. The former is our response to rich cuts of meat, for example, and is easy to understand. The latter can be found in subdued flavours, for example, in seasonal vegetables from which the bitterness has been removed, and is

Japanese culinary sensibility: think less, feel more

something that is felt, not thought. The good taste of Japanese food is something that is enjoyed using all of the five senses: sight, hearing, touch, smell and taste. It is a conscious expression of what we sense.

We talk about 'eating with your eyes': with Japanese cuisine, you can see by looking at the dish whether it will be delicious or not. I am not talking about food that has been decorated to appear beautiful. Our eyes, ears, skin, nose and mouth work together to perceive good taste. Here I am talking about the eyes as representatives of the parts of the body not directly involved in the act of eating. We hone our five senses and attempt to understand what the ingredients themselves are like.

Dishes that are prepared for formal occasions, such as the tea ceremony, provide an opportunity to taste with the five senses, taken to an extreme. This is an unusual setting, which allows you to concentrate on tasting food. The difference between everyday cooking, such as a soup and a side dish ('ke') and the food served in the tea ceremony ('haré') is that with the latter you do not mix different foods but savour the unique flavours and textures of individual items alongside the tea. In the food that accompanies the tea ceremony, even rice is served three times, in three ways that correspond to what you might call the

Rice, Miso Soup, Pickles

different stages of the rice's life: 'not-yet-steamed rice', 'well-ripened rice' and 'burnt rice in hot water'.

In everyday meals, there is always rice, and miso soup and side dishes are eaten either alternately or at the same time (what some call 'seasoning the rice inside your mouth'). However, in everyday meals we sometimes also enjoy tasting subtle and delicious flavours. Side dishes that might look like they do not go with rice at all can be placed on the table according to the seasons as an everyday treat. In spring, lightly cooked bamboo shoots or green peas, simmered to bring out their colour. In summer, slippery water shield. In autumn, charming *dobinmushi* (food steamed in an earthenware pot). In winter, warming boiled tofu ... Things like this bring a little 'nobility' into the day-to-day diet, and are another facet of Japanese home cooking.

In other words, Japanese people enjoy foods that engage the five senses, both in celebratory haré cooking as well as everyday ke dishes. In view of this, I would like to consider what it is like to taste with each of the five senses using examples from celebratory food. Again, these are things that can be found in everyday food too.

Sight

You cannot eat sashimi that has been exposed to the wind; if something has lost its freshness, you will perceive it with your eyes. Tofu is white and has distinct corners, giving it a neat shape: if you place a rectangular piece of tofu on a round plate, you can create a light and beautiful dish by adding some chopped spring onions and a little grated ginger. But what do we actually see there? You might see someone and say that they are 'good-looking' or 'look lovely'. When we do that, we are not just referring to the beauty we see with our eyes, we are talking about that person's behaviour and speech, which reflect their inner self, about everything together. In the same way, we see the good flavour of food or raw ingredients in their appearance, before we taste them. Our sensitivity allows us to perceive their beauty: we use our experience to see more than what we are actually looking at, there on the plate. We can see it with this type of food because it is not highly processed and brings out the best in its ingredients.

When soft and fragile tofu or fresh sashimi are arranged on a plate, the amount of work that has gone into producing these things is clearly evident. Even though these dishes are served raw, we know they will be safe to eat. Because they are beautiful, we instinctively feel that we can trust them.

Likewise, with high-quality Japanese confectionery, individual items can be made with almost identical ingredients, but based on their seasonal appearance and the image they create, we can tell (just by looking) that they will taste different.

Hearing

First, try to imagine the sound of cooking. The sound you hear from the kitchen is the sound of something delicious being made. Just hearing it can put you in a happy mood. When cooking sounds good, it can be a sign that the right temperature for creating delicious flavours has been reached. By contrast, sounds that make you feel uncomfortable can be a sign that something has gone wrong or got burnt. For example, when you crack an egg into a frying pan, if the temperature of the pan is just right, it will make a pleasant sizzling sound. That is the sound of the egg frying properly. If the pan is too hot and you hear a short, sharp sound like an 'ouch', it means the egg has burnt and will taste bitter, and if the pan is made of iron, it will also stick.

There are many delicious sounds that come from the kitchen. If you put aromatic, toasted sesame seeds

Japanese culinary sensibility: think less, feel more

into an earthenware mortar, and grind them with a pestle made from the hard wood of the Japanese pepper tree, it makes a very good sound. Water boiling in an iron kettle hanging over a traditional Japanese hearth, miso soup simmering in a saucepan: these are also lovely sounds.

The beautiful sounds heard in a tearoom or living room during the tea ceremony tend to stand out against the stillness. You hear the sound of the wind soughing through pine needles, the sound of insects, the sound of people serving tea in a calm and beautiful way, or the sound of the *shamisen* (a traditional three-stringed instrument resembling a lute) reverberating against the silence. The sentiments associated with a comfortable sound appear out of the silence. A beautiful sound is set in contrast to the absence of sound.

Touch

Onomatopoeia and phenomimes are often used in Japanese. *Korikori* (munching on something like a cucumber), *karikari* (crunching on some crispy bacon), *sakusaku* (crunching on a delicate biscuit), *garigari* (munching on something hard like a carrot), *tsurutsuru* (slurping some noodles) ... these are sounds we make when we eat certain foods, but they also express the way different foods feel in our mouths. In Japanese, we can share the nuances of these slightly different sensations quite accurately using onomatopoeia.

In Japanese cuisine, we can enjoy a whole range of different textures, arguably a much wider range than in foreign cuisine. For example, the gentle slurping noise we make when we eat *zarusoba* (chilled buckwheat noodles served in a bamboo basket with dipping sauce and toppings) is an expression of how good the noodles feel when we swallow them, and is necessary in order to enjoy them. Even though the sound of other people eating is inherently unpleasant, making this sound is generally accepted – in fact, it is considered a sign of appreciation.

The temperature of food is another kind of stimulation, and therefore also appeals to the sense of touch. Personally, I like things that are so hot I need to blow on them and things that are so icy they give me a headache but if something is too hot or too cold, it becomes impossible for the tastebuds to detect how that food is supposed to taste. Consequently, you might say that we are sacrificing flavour in order to prioritise the sense of touch. This may seem surprising, but I think in Japanese cuisine we can be quite vague about taste as perceived by the tastebuds and generally give it less importance. In Western cuisine, I do not think texture and temperature are enjoyed to quite the same degree. There, the range of temperatures at which food is considered delicious is much narrower because taste and smell come first. One might even say that Japanese cuisine gives greater importance to appearance and texture than many other types of cooking.

Smell

When we smell something unpleasant, we tend to turn our faces away; when there is a pleasant fragrance, we bring our noses closer to it. The fine smell of *oden* (a stew consisting of fish cakes, boiled eggs, daikon radish and other things simmered in a light broth) and the broth served with buckwheat *soba* noodles stimulate the appetite. Good smells produced during cooking are evidence of delicious food being made. By contrast, fish that is no longer fresh or anything that is rotting will always be accompanied by a bad smell. When you write *nioi* (smell) in Japanese, there are actually two different *kanji* or logographic characters to choose from, depending on whether the smell is good or bad.

If we see some food and think it looks a little suspicious, we may decide whether or not it is safe by smelling it. Unpleasant odours can be spread by saprophytic bacteria circulating in the air or released from an environment where they can multiply, so we are suspicious of bad smells and take their absence as a good sign. Garlic and Chinese chives, which have a lingering fragrance (or smell), are avoided in the food used in the tea ceremony. This may be connected to our general love of cleanliness, but in this context, we find peace of mind when there is no smell at all. If the delicate fragrance of *kinome* (the leaf bud of a Japanese pepper tree) or yuzu fleetingly appears where there was no smell before and then disappears again, we perceive them as beautiful smells.

Taste

In everyday food, the strong tastes of Korean barbecue, some Chinese dishes and certain types of Western cuisine seem to have an immediate effect on the body, giving us a wholly pleasant sensation, which we perceive as good taste. I think this type of good taste can even mitigate stress. The pleasure of rewarding your colleagues for their hard work by treating them to a meal somewhere is perhaps the modern equivalent of

Japanese culinary sensibility: think less, feel more

a celebration day meal, and these foods with strong flavours are popular choices. This type of good taste is easy to grasp and enjoy. The taste of Japanese cuisine, however, is much more subtle. It requires a special sensitivity that people who are used to this cuisine develop.

One of the guiding principles of Japanese cuisine is to get the best out of the ingredients used. If you were to ask me where that refined taste lies, I would say it is in the nucleus of the raw ingredients, from which any bitterness and astringent taste and colour, other than white, has been removed. The reason that we turn unpolished rice into white rice, and polish the surface of the rice used to make *ginjō* sake (high-quality sake brewed by low temperature fermentation from white rice milled to 60%) is based on the same idea. A subtle, refined and beautiful flavour (or fragrance) emerges that could not even have been sensed when the other, miscellaneous smells and flavours were still there.

We wash fish in cold water (removing their scales, gills, guts and blood and wiping away all the excess moisture) and peel the edible skin from vegetables. There is a strong umami flavour as well as nutritional value in these things, but there are also miscellaneous flavours and smells and even toxins.

Japanese culinary sensibility means removing and disposing of these things and eating only the beautiful part.

In Chinese and Western cuisine, the intestines and blood of a pig are not wasted but processed into sausages and other products for human consumption. In Japan, however, one eats little other than the muscle; the entrails of a fish (together with its head and bones) are not used on festive occasions but only in everyday cooking. It is a question of making the absolute best of already beautiful things, and at the same time, throwing away anything that is considered unnecessary. The Japanese have a global reputation for eschewing waste, but in fact Japanese people can also be surprisingly wasteful. Perhaps the distinction made long ago between clean and unclean, the discovery that things were either pure or impure, ensured that the habit of attributing absolute values to everything became deeply rooted in our subconscious. After all, a light that shines brightly creates a deep darkness. Because we looked for an uncommon purity in things, darkness appeared, and before we became conscious of it, we felt the duality of the two extremes to be inextricably linked, and as an unconscious act, we started to treat both of these things as being inevitable. I think that by acknowledging this duality within ourselves and not averting our gaze, and thinking of it consciously, we can retain the rare nobility inherent in our traditional culture.

Japanese cuisine avoids anything cloudy and values things that are clean and clear. If something goes well, we say *sumimashita* (literally, 'I have made it clear/clean/transparent'). If something does not go well, we apologise, saying *sumimasen* (literally, 'It is not clear/clean/transparent'). If you are sitting around a *naberyōri* (a style of cooking where meat, fish and vegetables are cooked in a hot pot, usually placed in the middle of the table, with people helping themselves straight from the pot), then someone will invariably skim off the scum that forms on the surface of the broth. This removes the toxins: it is a kind of detoxification process. There is one school of thought that believes that anything with a high nutritional value should be eaten whole. Another approach, which is inherent to Japanese cuisine, cautions against putting anything in one's mouth that might harm the body. For this reason, with things that have been cooked properly using the traditional techniques of Japanese cuisine, there is only a low risk that they will go off. If this is combined with the theory and techniques of modern hygiene management, it is even healthier.

Rice, Miso Soup, Pickles

Bringing out the true nature of the raw ingredients used by removing their bitterness and making them clean and clear is an expression of the taste that Japanese people tend to love most of all. This is why the words *kireaji* (a sharp, crisp and clean aftertaste), *sukkiri* (clean and refreshing) and *karomi* (lightness) are used so often to express the taste of washoku.

In Japanese, sculpting a statue of the Buddha from a single tree is known as 'negative' sculpture, while producing a statue by adding clay is known as 'positive' sculpture. In this sense, washoku is a kind of 'negative' cuisine. When we remove any bitterness, we sometimes also lose some, if not all, of the taste and nutritional value, but we make a point of not adding any additional flavour. We prize a clear broth because there is no added flavour, but instead, a taste texture known as umami. The absence of a taste that one can perceive with the tastebuds is more than made up for by the visual pleasure of 'eating with the eyes' and the sense of touch.

The cuisine of the Jōmon period

Approximately 7 million years ago, our ancestors stood on two feet, became able to use their hands freely, and broke away from the anthropoid apes. About 3 million years ago, they picked up stones, the first tools, used them to crush meat in order to soften it, and ate it. About 1.6 million years ago, they made other stones into weapons and learnt how to work together to hunt game. Then, about 800,000 years ago, they started using fire.

If you have fire, the nights are bright and warm and you can keep away the cold as well as any wild animals. This is probably why, when we see a fire burning today, it makes us feel relaxed and safe. If you hold a lump of meat in a fire, it will sizzle and smell good, and become soft enough to chew with your teeth.

Rice, Miso Soup, Pickles

When people learnt how to produce earthenware, it meant they could cook with heat – roasting, boiling and steaming their food – and they could include a much wider range of fruits, nuts, berries and plants in their diet than before. Because they could now cut up, mash and cook their raw ingredients, their food was easier to swallow and easier to digest, and they no longer needed to spend many hours chewing their food like apes.

In his book *Catching Fire: How Cooking Made Us Human* (Profile Books, 2009), Richard Wrangham, a biological anthropologist at Harvard University, argues that human beings became human because they cooked. In fact, he explains the process of evolution from apes such as gorillas and chimpanzees to humans through the act of cooking. Since the food they ate was softer, because it had been cooked, they no longer needed such large jaws for chewing, and their faces took on a neater, more delicate appearance. The food that was now easier to digest no longer required such a large digestive tract and so their stomachs shrank and their bodies became more streamlined. When they began cooking their food, our ancestors began to take on a more human appearance.

The time that had to be spent on food and digestion was significantly shortened thanks to cooking and,

The cuisine of the Jōmon period

for the first time, people might have had spare time. They would also have needed less energy to digest their food; this spare energy was used by the body to create larger brains, and this resulted in intellectual development. From the beginning, early humans had been at a disadvantage with respect to animals, since they were less physically capable, and generally weaker and slower. But with their larger, more well-developed brains, they learnt to use words and communicate, learnt how to cooperate with each other, and became the most successful living things on the planet.

Vessels with traces of cooking have been discovered among the earthenware produced in the Jōmon period, approximately 15,000 years ago.* Archaeologists believe that these vessels were made by women, so women may also have used them for cooking. The women of the Jōmon period probably went to nearby estuaries, hills and fields to looks for things that were edible, picking up shells and gathering wild plants

---

* The earthenware currently thought to be the oldest in the world is something made around 18,000 years ago and excavated in Hunan Province, China. Other fragments that were, until recently, thought to be the oldest in the world are from a piece of Jōmon period earthenware produced around 16,000 years ago that was dug up in the archaeological site at Ōdai Yamamoto, Aomori Prefecture, Japan.

Rice, Miso Soup, Pickles

and bamboo shoots in spring; picking fruit in summer; gathering nuts, harvesting mushrooms and digging up potatoes in winter. Physically strong and curious men would have gathered in groups, communicated with each other, and gone deep into the sea or the mountains, travelling significant distances to track and catch their game. They would probably have brought home what they caught, skinned it, not letting any part of it go to waste, given thanks, roasted the meat and then shared it with their companions and their families.

According to archaeologist Tatsuo Kobayashi, one of the reasons why the culture of the Jōmon period lasted for more than 10,000 years is that, by eating different kinds of food at different times of year, they were able to eliminate the risk of famine. I imagine that the women of this period carefully washed the food that had been gathered before putting it in an earthenware vessel with boiling water. Perhaps they thought they were using magical tools to work on the sacred fire. I imagine that it must have been very difficult to turn something inedible into something edible. They may have thought that creating delicious food was something wonderful and mysterious that humans could not even take credit for. And then they carefully divided the warming soup among all the members of their family.

The cuisine of the Jōmon period

The special feature of dishes that are cooked in a pot is that you can fill many stomachs and warm many bodies with just a small quantity of meat. It is quite different to cooking meat you have caught by holding it over a fire. Many people can eat something that has been boiled, unlike roast meat that just serves a few. Roasting and cooking meat is something luxurious, and this is why even today, in many parts of the world, a 'roast' is still considered a treat, a carnival dish. A warm vegetable soup, by contrast, is a staple at home in many places, appearing on restaurant menus and in the school canteen. For many people, warm vegetable soup is an important, reassuring dish. Even today, if you are invited to someone's house for dinner in many Western countries, it may be the husband or the father who will cook, carve and serve the roast, but it will be the mother who makes the warm vegetable soup using a pot. Perhaps mothers and fathers have always had their own dishes that they cook and serve.

Our ancestors probably made soups and stews in earthenware pots more than 10,000 years ago. Even now in Japan, when winter comes, hot pots are very popular. When I was a child, I remember people being strict about table manners. There was always a 'hot pot boss', that is, someone in charge of cooking and serving the hot pot. In Japanese cuisine, we distinguish between soups and stews: soups have always been more of an everyday food, while meals cooked together around a pot were for celebrations. I once saw a historical recreation where reconstructed Jōmon period vessels were used to cook the food thought to have been eaten at that time, and the ingredients were cooked all mixed together, but I think this was a mistake. I feel sure that the people of that time carefully cooked the raw ingredients that they had gathered one by one. In modern times, we aim to create delicious things when we cook, and we cook things one by one because it brings out the flavour of our raw ingredients, but I think they would have done so because they treasured their ingredients. Not jumbling them up resulted in a more delicious taste. If they had mixed everything up, I do not think the refined Japanese cuisine we have today could ever have developed. It is hard to imagine that our cuisine became refined over the course of time; there are many reasons why I think it was refined from the very beginning.

Japanese cuisine was not born out of the technological progress of humans. Traditionally, all of the raw ingredients made by *otentosama*, the 'almighty sun' (that watched over everything like a sacred

The cuisine of the Jōmon period

being), were inhabited by *kami*, or sacred spirits, and so one treated them with respect; if not, one would have been punished. Since the ingredients were sacred, I think people would have washed first, touched them only with clean hands, and cooked them one by one. Our food culture was born out of fear and respect for nature as well as the climate, and out of an awareness for what is sacred.

We are talking about a time before there was a distinction between food that tasted good or bad.* This was how I imagine the relationship with raw ingredients might have been when people first started to cook – then, as time went by, and people became more conscious of what they were eating, they began to make good taste a criterion for good food, and gradually became more creative. However, innovation was always very cautious, as it should continue to be.

---

* A time before there was a distinction between food that tasted good or bad ... Muneyoshi Yanagi, founder of the *mingei* (folk art) movement, uses the Buddhist idea behind the fourth of Amida Buddha's forty-eight vows, 'If I were to have a conflict between beauty and ugliness in the Pure Land, I would not become a Buddha,' to explain the beauty of well bowls used for the tea ceremony, which are regarded 'without the distinction of beauty or ugliness.'

Rice, Miso Soup, Pickles

I cannot think of a cuisine in any other part of Asia, or indeed the rest of the world, where washing one's hands first is so fundamental. Even though scientific learning is traditionally thought to have reached Japan from other countries, the fact that this aspect of food culture is particular to Japan suggests that it might have originated here. It was something that already existed in these solitary islands* before people arrived from the mainland bringing writing, scholarship, rice cultivation and ironware.

---

* An expression used to mean the ancient island nation of Japan in *Nijugengokokka Nihon* ('Dual Language Nation Japan') by Kyūyō Ishikawa (Nihon Hōsō Shuppan Kyōkai, 2011)

Cleanliness

From what we know today, the people of these solitary islands in Asia (Japan) feared and revered nature, worshipped all the deities, avoided fighting, trusted and were familiar with their natural surroundings, and lived a modest life. According to the *Gishiwajinden*, a chronicle of Chinese history compiled around the end of the third century AD (and the first foreign book to describe Japan in recognisable detail), in a chapter dedicated to Japan, the early Japanese were 'polite and clean'.

After this, times changed and there was war, but I personally believe we still carry a fragment of the spirit of those early Jōmon people within us today. They did not have writing as we understand it today, and so nothing remains in the way of documentation, but I would like to give a few examples of things that are thought to have been passed down to us from that period.

Rice, Miso Soup, Pickles

We wash our hands when we come home, we wash our hands before we cook, we wash our hands before we eat. The custom of removing our shoes before stepping 'up' into the house (as one does in most Japanese homes) is another aspect of this: when we come in from the outside, we are crossing a threshold, entering a space where the kami, or sacred spirits, are enshrined.

When chopsticks are placed sideways on the table, between the person and their food, they create a boundary between man and nature, between the blessings of otentosama, the bountiful sun, and the person who is about to receive them. Before we eat, we say *itadakimasu* (a phrase that literally means, 'I humbly receive,' but that is a way of giving thanks to all the people involved in the production and preparation of the food one is about to eat), and I think that with this word we dissolve the sacred boundary.

I also think that picking up a tea bowl or soup bowl in one's hands in order to drink or eat is a custom that goes back to the Jōmon period, before the arrival of rice cultivation. We are told that chopsticks came over to Japan from the mainland together with the spoon, as a set, at some point during the Asuka period (c.550–710 AD), but in Japan we use chopsticks on their own, without a spoon. When we have soup, we pick up the

Cleanliness

soup bowl, hold it up to our mouth, and drink straight from the bowl.

Arranging chopsticks horizontally, in front of our food, and picking up our bowls to eat, are customs that are particular to Japan. In cooking, we value clear soup from which the astringent taste has been removed, and when we eat the ingredients from a hot pot, we enjoy them one by one, when they are ready: these things all seem to be peculiar to the Japanese way of eating.

And then there is sashimi. Sashimi is not the same as raw fish. We cannot eat fish raw just because it is fresh. After a fish has been caught, it is treated with great care: the guts and scales are removed, it is washed in cold water and carefully dried. It is then filleted and the bones and skin are removed. It is cut into beautiful pieces using a very sharp knife, and finally arranged on the plate so as to create a miniature landscape. A clear distinction is made between the different stages of work, and usually the working area is purified in between one stage and the next: this is because the fish is not thought of simply as an ingredient.

In Japanese, there are two different characters for writing *tsukuru* (the verb 'to make'): one is reserved for things like sake brewing and miso fermentation

▼ Rice, Miso Soup, Pickles

that a person cannot do by themselves. Sashimi is also 'made' like this, that is, not quite by the human hand. This is because fish are believed to be sacred, and people once thought that when we return their souls to the sacred spirits, we receive the blessing of their flesh in return. The same belief is reflected in the ritual of *iomante* or *kuma-okuri* ('bear sending-off'), the ancient custom that was traditionally observed by the Ainu (an indigenous people from the north of Japan) when they caught and ritually killed a bear, before they could eat its meat.

From our modern-day perspective, the shells of shellfish are nothing more than leftovers and can simply be thrown away, but for the people of the past, a shell mound was a sending-off place, somewhere where the souls that had given them blessings could be laid to rest.

It is possible that details like this, which have been passed down from the Jōmon period, are preserved in our sensitivity to waste and our love of cleanliness and purity, in the distinctions that we have inherited from the distant past. When we deal with something, we refer to it as *shimatsu suru*, literally 'to start and finish', because we first purify the place where we are working and make it clean before starting again. This practice is still a custom today, and in manufacturing produces goods that are particularly precise. It takes more than manual dexterity to produce beautiful things.

We use the word *kirei* very frequently in daily life. In Japanese, 'kirei' means both 'beautiful' *and* 'clean', and we also use it to describe 'honest' work. Truth without lies, delicious food produced selflessly, beauty without blemish, those things that are held up as human ideals, 'the true, the good and the beautiful'. The Japanese express all this in the single word, 'kirei'.

(Re)discovering Japanese Food

和食を初期化する

Time to nurture the mind

I was born in 1957 and when I was a child, you could walk along the alleys in the evening and the smell of dinner being prepared would waft out of every house. At that time, it was taken for granted that housewives would cook every day. One day, it had got quite late by the time my mother went out to do the shopping, and so she hurried to the market saying, 'I'm so embarrassed to be doing my shopping in the afternoon.' When she got home again, I remember her washing some greens at the sink by the well (was this all that was left at the market?), putting them in a sieve and then covering them with a cloth. She would simmer them briefly before supper. There was barely anything in the fridge, since in those days the custom of stocking up was unheard of: food shopping was simply something you did every day. There was also a sense of guilt associated with ordering food from a meal delivery service. Ordering

Rice, Miso Soup, Pickles

takeaway udon or *donburi* (cooked rice, topped with various ingredients, served in a large bowl) at the home of relatives who worked in business was a rare occasion for excitement.

Cooking was a job for women, and even though my father (Masaru Doi, a famous food researcher) was a food researcher, it would have been impossible to imagine him going shopping and bringing home a bag of vegetables. At primary school, I was teased for having a cookery teacher for a father. This was the time when a man was not supposed to enter the kitchen alone, and even my father, as the head of the family, very rarely did any cooking at home.

The road outside our house was unpaved, and whenever it rained there would be puddles everywhere. There were hardly any cars, either, so we often played catch in front of the house. When school finished, children of all ages would gather there. Children would go home, drop off their school bags, and then head straight out to play. Our playground was anywhere outside the house.

I remember we played hide-and-seek and tag in vacant lots that were given names as if they were foreign territories. We would put on the baseball caps of the teams we supported, the Nankai Hawks or the Hanshin Tigers, and play 'triangular baseball' with a rubber ball. Or wrestle in the sandpit, trying out different moves on each other. The girls often played jumping games with a long loop of elastic. After we had played all we could, I remember how content I felt, and how delicious supper tasted after having a refreshing bath. In the 1950s, televisions were still black and white.

From around that time, exotic Western things began to appear in our house one by one. Sometimes breakfast would be toast and tea with milk. Cheese omelettes, grapefruit halves or a salad made from crunchy lettuce cut into wedges, which we would eat with salt. When the filling in the Christmas cake (a light sponge cake, layered with cream and strawberries, traditionally eaten at Christmas in Japan) changed from the usual buttercream to fresh whipped cream, I thought it was the most delicious thing I had ever tasted. I can still remember my delight when, in the first year of middle school (I would have been about 12 or 13), I first ate battered prawns with tartar sauce at a hotel.

But although there were so many new things to eat, our daily diet was still essentially Japanese. Even in the house I grew up in, where one of my parents was

Rice, Miso Soup, Pickles

a food researcher, we had almost exclusively Japanese cuisine. If we ever had meat prepared with butter or oil or other Western food, it was an unusual and happy occasion and so I remember it well. We could not afford to eat as luxuriously as we do now, but somehow it was a peaceful and happy time. I think it was this childhood that gave me a Japanese sensibility for food.

When I got home, I would take off my shoes and tidy them away. Of course, I would wash my hands, and sometimes I would even have to wash my feet. Say 'please' and 'thank you' my mother would say. 'Sit up straight to eat!' I remember there were separate cloths for wiping the table and washing up. I learnt to tell right from left because chopsticks are held in your right hand, while a rice bowl is held in your left. I would get scolded with an 'Elbows off the table!' If we had bad posture, it was 'No slouching.' Side dishes were served in small individual dishes. We were not allowed to leave a single grain of rice in our bowls. I can still hear my mother's voice saying, 'Hold your bowl in both hands when I give you seconds!' My father would chime in, 'When you've finished your rice, rinse out the bowl with a bit of tea!' Even though family mealtimes were happy, there were various rules we had to follow.

Every year, everyone would welcome spring, chasing the cherry blossoms, and when autumn came, pay attention to the changing colours. Our pet fish would lay their eggs, and we would listen out for the first of the autumn cicadas that signalled the changing of the seasons. If an exciting excursion was planned, I would worry about the weather, making a *teruterubōzu* (a traditional weather charm to hang in the window), and then head off, equipped with a packed lunch my mother had made me.

The seasonality of ingredients was all around us: when we saw tomatoes in the greengrocer's storefront, we would be happy because it would be almost the summer holidays. Later on in summer, the green and red of discarded watermelon peel would be conspicuous among the rubbish. As soon as the first fruit of each season went on sale, we would go out and buy it. At Sports Day in the autumn (a public holiday held annually on the second Monday in October), the first green-skinned mandarins would taste sour but delicious. If I was ever given sweets, I would always make an offering to sacred spirits or the Buddha at the household shrine before eating them myself. If I caught a cold, I would be given okayu (rice porridge) and pickled plums. My mother would boil spinach, roll it up with a

Rice, Miso Soup, Pickles

sushi mat and serve it in a small bowl with soy sauce flavoured with sesame seeds ground in a mortar and, finally, red pickled ginger or a large serving of yuzu.

The Japanese sense of beauty

On the evenings when I heard the sound of a small bell in the street, I would take a bowl and go out to buy tofu from the travelling tofu seller. The tofu would be stored in cold, clean water and have straight, clean edges. In summer, we would eat it chilled; in winter, boiled. Any mother could probably have cut the tofu neatly on the palm of her hand, slid it into a saucepan full of hot water and dissolved miso in it to make soup. On special days when we ate sushi, there would be *osuimono* (a light and delicate soup with a clear broth) with diced tofu and bundles of *mitsuba* (Japanese parsley). This special, clear soup was only made on days that were different to the others in some way.

At a tofu shop, one cannot sell tofu if the corners are broken, not even at half price. One used to hear of tofu sellers who, on seeing a child from a poor

Rice, Miso Soup, Pickles

family entering the shop, would deliberately break the corners off a piece of tofu so that it could no longer be sold and give it to them. People even used to say rude things like 'I hope you hit your head on a corner of tofu and die.' For us, it has always been important for tofu to have clean corners, even though they have nothing to do with the taste: it is important for it to be square and beautiful. This is the Japanese sense of beauty.

If you cut a traditional block of tofu in two, it became a cube, and this looked beautiful on a round plate. If you cut it on the diagonal, you would get a nice triangle, and if you cut half a block into four, you would get the cubes used for boiled tofu. The tofu you can buy now is always pre-packaged, and at some point the standard shape changed so that you no longer get a cube when you cut it in half; and if you turn it over, it now bears the imprint of the packaging. The tofu can still be sold, even if the corners are broken inside the package, not because our aesthetic standards have changed but because this is judged to be acceptable provided the best-before date has not passed and the packaging is not damaged. In this way, one by one, the beautiful things disappear.

In the Japan of my childhood, I think there were still many things like this in our daily lives that were

The Japanese sense of beauty

distinctly Japanese. I think the fact that people worked as hard as they could, even when they were poor, provided the foundation for the high-performance products that supported Japan's rapid economic growth. It went without saying that craftsmen would create products that were well-made throughout, even on the side that could not be seen, because they knew the work that went into the back would eventually be seen from the front. I think they were able to respond effectively to the periods of extreme change because everything that they learnt at this time gave them the criteria to live and work by. Because everyone had their own criteria for relating to things and seeing things, they were able to ascertain and judge whatever they looked at without needing any further instructions.

I think anyone who had a childhood similar to me, and any young person who grew up in a traditional Japanese home or place, will be able to understand both the Japan of yesterday and the Japan of today. As Norinaga Motoori (an influential philosopher and intellectual who lived in the nineteenth century) argued, I think every Japanese person has an innate capacity to understand '*mono no aware*' (that is, an awareness of the impermanence of things and both a wistfulness at their passing and a sadness that this state is a fact of life). It is because they have acquired an ability to understand and sympathise with other people's feelings, by observing the changes in nature and the state of things, that they can sense Japan's true beauty. In our modern society, technological development has given birth to a new civilisation and the environment has changed significantly, but I believe that any young person growing up today will have somehow inherited a seed of this ability to perceive beauty.

Changes in food

In the post-war period, Japanese people tended to be physically smaller than people in Europe or the United States, and this was thought to have been due to nutritional deficiency. At around the same time, the idea of moving to a diet that included more bread rather than rice, as well as milk and meat, which is high in protein, began to spread. Moreover, around the end of the 1950s, there was a theory that rice was somehow damaging to intellectual development – I remember this from my early childhood. Also at that time, aid was received from the United States for the import of flour and skimmed milk powder for school lunches under the pretext of supplying 'Food for Peace' (although this was actually a trade strategy to use up surplus US produce). The policy of providing a complete meal consisting of bread, milk and a side dish was introduced in 1950 and in some places continues to this day.

Rice, Miso Soup, Pickles

From around 1956, again under the auspices of improving the Japanese diet, a fleet of 'kitchen cars' (food demonstration buses, also sponsored by the US Department of Agriculture's Foreign Agricultural Service) started to drive around Japan. In what was known as the 'frying pan movement', trained housewives would use these mobile kitchen counters equipped with propane gas to demonstrate cooking methods using (surplus, American) cooking oil. At the time it was strange and unusual in all but the wealthiest families to cook deep-fried food and dishes using oil, but it was probably as a result of this initiative that dishes like fried rice, omelettes with mincemeat, vegetable *nitsuke* (a dish where the vegetables are first fried then boiled in a sauce containing sake, mirin, sugar and soy sauce) appeared in our homes.

In the 1960s, it became normal for young women to learn cookery as part of their preparation for married life, and there were more than 20,000 students in the cooking school that my father ran. If you look at photographs from that time, you can see young women crowded around the workstations vying with each other to master the new dishes, all beaming as they put their new skills into practice.

Changes in food

The people of the time probably felt a keen sense of joy as national recovery followed the bitterness of defeat in the Second World War. Individuals worked hard to realise their own dreams, afraid of being excluded from the country's rapid economic growth. They were most likely drawn to the American lifestyle with its big refrigerators and other US imports, and welcomed them into their homes.

I think what was different then was that when young women studied the basics of cooking, it was treated as a kind of general knowledge that everyone should acquire. The circumstances of the time probably did not make it easy to learn a new style of cooking, but I expect they absorbed the new skills and knowledge readily enough. What they learnt would have included basic Japanese cuisine as well as how to cook meat, Chinese dishes and Western dishes, and so a diet that was more richly varied and filling was introduced into their future homes.

Today we ask our families, 'Would you prefer to have meat or fish tonight?' When we do this, we are of course asking what they would like as a main dish, but this way of thinking of a meal in terms of a 'main dish' and a 'side dish' only started when the study of nutrition, which was gradually becoming established as a universal science at that time, arrived in Japan.

Rice, Miso Soup, Pickles

From a nutritional point of view, a main dish is something containing meat or fish, that is, something that will help the body to produce blood and muscle. A side dish is made of vegetables, something that supplements the main dish by providing vitamins and minerals. This pattern was applied to the traditional model of Japanese cuisine, consisting of one soup and one, two or three side dishes, and as a result, rice plus a main dish and two kinds of side dish became the new ideal meal.

In some ways, it makes sense to prioritise nutrition over culture and classify dishes according to their nutritional value, but it would be an oversimplification to treat food as nothing more than nutrition. Traditionally, Japan did not have this custom of distinguishing between more or less important dishes. They were all just dishes to accompany rice. If you were to ask me what had been the main dishes in Japan up until then, I can only think of fried fish and warm or chilled tofu. Today, 'side dishes' include things like *kiriboshi* (dried daikon strips) that contain fried tofu, or miso soup that contains miso and tofu. In other words, even if you refer to something as a 'side dish', it will often contain something that is actually a main dish, such as tofu or small amounts of meat. *Nikujaga*

Changes in food

(literally 'meat and potatoes', a dish of meat, potatoes, carrots and onions stewed in dashi, soy sauce, mirin and sugar) looks like it ought to be a main dish, but it usually contains lots of vegetables, which would make it a side dish. With Japanese dishes, there is often an overlap: there is simply no clear distinction between primary and secondary dishes.

However, when I make hamburgers as a main dish, it doesn't seem enough unless I prepare a side dish of kiriboshi and put meat in my miso soup as well, so this meal tends to be quite high in protein and fat. When recipes appear in cookery magazines these days, in response to readers' requests they are now accompanied by a nutrition-oriented calorie calculation, which is always set out according to a meat-based main dish and a vegetable-based side dish. The distinction is variously explained as being that between rich and light dishes, large and small dishes, etc.

The year 1958 saw the first sales of instant ramen. The United States and the Soviet Union had already embarked on their space exploration programmes, and at the time it was thought that the meals of the future would consist of convenience foods like space food. It later became apparent that food like this does not satisfy human appetite, so this did not turn out to be the case, and yet, it is a fact that almost all foods are now available for purchase in some instant, boil-in-the-bag or other convenient form.

In 1970, to coincide with the Osaka World Expo, Japan's first fast food outlet and first family restaurant were opened. That year is known as the first year of the modern restaurant industry in Japan. Following this, as a result of the booming economy, the number of restaurants increased quickly and the pleasure of dining out became an everyday thing.

Events that led to changes in Japanese food culture between 1950 and 1975

1950	The introduction of school lunches consisting of bread, milk and a side dish, resulting from the import of flour, etc. from the United States.
1956	The introduction of the 'frying pan movement' and the deployment of 'kitchen cars' as part of the campaign to improve nutrition (frying in oil becomes standard).

Changes in food

1958	First sales of instant ramen.
1964	Tokyo Olympics. Campaign to beautify the capital. Circular farming, which had been practised in Tokyo since the Edo period (human waste collected in the city is spread on the fields as fertiliser and then vegetables produced on the farms are supplied to the city in a sort of cycle between the urban and rural communities) gradually disappears.
c. 1965	Cookery schools to prepare young women for married life begin to spread.
1970	Osaka World Expo held. The first 'family restaurant' (a kind of informal, chain restaurant geared towards families and young people) is opened.
1975	The healthy 'Japanese-style diet' based on rice as a staple food and with a mixture of plant and animal products, etc. (i.e. a nutritionally well-balanced meal) is optimised, meaning that the average Japanese person has a healthier diet around this time than in earlier or later decades.

Rice, Miso Soup, Pickles

Although many of these changes were to be welcomed, they also caused various food and health-related problems in the years that followed, as well as some unexpected developments, for example:

- An increase in lifestyle-related disease (metabolic problems associated with a higher calorie diet, etc.).
- A decrease in rice consumption (this peaked in 1962 at 118kg per person per year, and by 2019 had fallen to less than half of that at 53kg per person per year).
- A decrease in miso consumption (in the past, each household would have allowed for one *to* (a traditional unit of measurement equivalent to around 18kg) for each family member, plus one *to* for guests as their annual stock. So, a person would have eaten around 18kg of miso per year. By 1968, annual consumption per person was around 7.6kg, and by 2019 this had dropped to around 3.7kg.
- A decrease in the national food autonomy ratio (calculated on a calorie basis, this was 73% in 1965 but had dropped to 38% by 2019).
- The amount of money spent on bread exceeds the amount spent on rice in a typical household (from around 2011).

What should I eat? What can I eat? What do I want to eat?

'What should I eat?'

'What can I eat?'

'What do I want to eat?'

I wonder how those of us living in Japan today would answer these three questions.

The answer to the question 'What should I eat?' is foods that have a high nutritional value and are good for you. The answer to the question 'What can I eat?' is food that is safe and secure. The answer to the question 'What do I want to eat?' will be different for everyone, but I imagine it is generally Korean barbecue, sushi and things like that. The reason why we do not eat this type of thing every day, other than the financial one, is probably that we know it would be bad for our health. It is nice to have a bit of a feast as a treat after working very hard, but the day after we eat too much, we might decide to eat nothing at all. If we have an annual health check, and the results are poor, then our dietary habits might come under scrutiny, and we might try an extreme diet to reduce the amount we eat. In modern society, we reflect and make conscious decisions about what we will and will not eat at different times, according to different conditions and our personal circumstances.

It is one thing going through this process for oneself, but when it comes to making decisions for the family, it is much more complicated. When you need to think of an appropriate menu for every meal, every day, it can become quite stressful. Moreover, there is now an enormous volume of information about food in the media, particularly on the television and on social media in Japan, and even if you try not to hear or see it, if you are living in modern society it is impossible to block it out – its influence is inescapable. Your mind knows that by eating something tasty, you will be able to relieve this stress, at least temporarily. You know that if you eat flour-based foods such as bread or pasta, which are easy to digest, your blood sugar level will rise straight away and you will feel better. It is a kind of conditioned reflex: just seeing foods like these makes us want to eat them.

Since when has it been like this, I wonder? What was it like 30 years ago, before we had mobile phones? Certainly, 50 years ago it would have been unnecessary to ask 'What should I eat? What can I eat? What do I want to eat?' The answer to all of these questions would have been the same: you ate what was there. The food that has nourished all ethnic groups over countless centuries may be simple, but it is nutritious, safe and delicious. We tend to think that, in times gone by, people did well to get by on such simple fare alone, because they did not know any better, but I am sure this is not the case. People have always known the difference when it comes to food.

I feel sure that people knew how to distinguish between special haré food and everyday ke food: everyday food is humble, and I think our bodies know that living from the minimum amount of food necessary is not only good for mind and body but also more comfortable. The successful merchants of pre-war Osaka who understood the meaning of luxury knew this, as did Ichiro Suzuki, the Major League baseball legend. Ascetic monks knew it, and so did students preparing to take examinations.

Rice, Miso Soup, Pickles

When people face challenges, they need to live like this, eating a humble diet, otherwise they cannot do their best. Eating is always pleasurable, but if you go too far, it leads to illness and a lack of mental focus. By making a clear distinction between the everyday and the celebratory, successful merchants and monks, students and sports stars of the past could ensure this did not happen. They would have lived modestly and cautioned against excess.

Reclaiming the model of Japanese cuisine

When I look around my home, I wonder whether there is still anything 'Japanese' about the way we live in Japan today. There are fewer rooms in our houses with traditional *tatami* mats, and we tend to sit on chairs now rather than on the floor. In modern cities, it has become very rare to see wooden pillars incorporated into rooms or earthen *tsuchikabe* walls. *Fusuma* sliding doors, paper-covered *shōji* that only let in a soft light and *tokonoma* alcoves for displaying calligraphy and flower arrangements have practically disappeared. Where are the Japanese features that we can still see and touch?

Just because they have become so rare, I do not think it means that Japanese people have all adopted a Western lifestyle. When they come home, they take off their shoes, making a clear distinction between the world outside and the home inside. The next thing many people do is wash their hands; they wash them again before they eat. With their inherent sense of cleanliness, they maintain something of the Japanese lifestyle through the way they behave. I believe that this type of behaviour, accompanied by a love of nature, allows us to keep something 'Japanese' in our hearts.

Even if we adopt a Western lifestyle and surround ourselves with Western-style things, in the middle of it all we are still Japanese. Japanese art still has its own unique quality, and in science and technology, Japanese products are sometimes better than their Western counterparts. This is not because of any kind of racial superiority, but I think it might have something to do with our emotional way of looking at things.

By emotion, here, I am referring to '*mono no aware*', that Japanese concept that translates as a compassion for things, or a sensitivity to things that are impermanent and a sadness at their passing. To be emotional, here, means to be in harmony with the four seasons, the changes in nature, as new life is born and old life decays, as these things affect us all. As I mentioned earlier, I think *mono no aware* is deeply integrated into our culture. In other countries, this sensitivity may have been lost long ago, but I think we have inherited it from our ancestors: Norinaga Motoori called it the 'ancient human mind'. I would like to believe we still retain a fragment of this ancient mind today. It is hard to express clearly, but I think it is at the centre of what many people perceive to be 'Japanese'.

A philosophy is emerging in Japan about what it really means to be Japanese, and this is what otentosama, the watchful sun, shows us: it is an absolute, something that must be followed as an ancient custom, something that has been inherited. However, now that we can no longer bear this in mind at all times, we take this vague notion that we cannot explain in words to be '*Japaneseness*', without thinking about it too deeply. Perhaps we prefer to focus on the plethora of new things and ideas that come from overseas.

But Japan has used foreign ideas, especially in science and technology, as the basis for many of its own innovations, and when we have faced difficulties, we have been able to resolve and overcome them because we persevered with determination and used our intuition. This resulted in the growth we have today. I think a 'Japanese' quality can be seen in this use of intuition and innovation. This has been useful

Rice, Miso Soup, Pickles

in many areas, for example, in the way the chief brewer at a sake brewery creates delicious sake.

I hope that in the future we will not lose this graceful, beautiful quality. How should we go about preserving it? I think the key is to have a structure in your daily life that allows for emotional enrichment and well-being: establishing a good foundation for your daily life. For food, which is the cornerstone of our daily lives, I think it is important to use the model of Japanese cuisine. I think this is what it means to pass Japanese cuisine on to future generations. If this also happens to coincide with what makes us happy and healthy, then it is a fine thing indeed.

Rather appropriately, the author Kyūyō Ishikawa shows us one good way of being Japanese in his book *Nijugengokokka Nihon* ('Dual Language Nation Japan'), which I mentioned earlier:

> The reason that the men and women of the Meiji Period had such a resolute attitude was not because they had 'Japanese spirit imbued with Western learning' or because they had 'Japanese spirit imbued with Chinese learning', but because, in addition to the Japanese mind and the Chinese spirit, they had Western learning, which actively embraced Western culture and ideas. In this sense,

the 'resolution' of Meiji man was perhaps another name for what we call 'qualifications' in modern man ... Through the reconstruction of the Japanese language, which has this three-dimensional structure made up of 'Japanese mind, Chinese spirit and Western learning', I think that we must strive to acquire a language that will be able to describe the ideas of the world at large.

In this passage, Ishikawa recognises that the language of Japan is a 'dual language', an amalgam of elements from the solitary islands and from the mainland (Japanese is written with a mixture of *kanji*, Chinese characters or ideograms, and *hiragana*, a cursive phonetic script, together with *katakana*, a more angular phonetic script used for writing foreign loanwords). He goes on to try to show how, in addition to the Japanese mind and Chinese spirit, we need to master the universal concepts of philosophy and create a new language for the Japanese.

Returning to the subject of Japanese cuisine, which was recently registered as an Intangible Cultural Heritage by UNESCO, it is not all good news, since it is currently considered to be an endangered species. I think that in order to make it accessible and universal, as well as something we can be proud of again, we need to understand the current situation and, instead of leaving things vague and undefined, put it into words, pass it on and put it into practice.

I want to try and think of the current state of Japanese cuisine in terms of the ideas used in 'Dual Language Nation Japan'. The 'Japanese mind' is the idea of getting the best out of nature's raw materials, and always trying to find harmony – Japanese food as represented by the dishes of the tea ceremony. The 'Chinese spirit' is celebratory food such as chirashi-zushi (literally 'scattered sushi', a colourful dish where rice is mixed with vinegar and various other things such as sashimi, cooked and shredded egg, bamboo and nori are scattered on top) where the raw ingredients are mixed together, or food we eat on a daily basis made with the cooking techniques from mainland Asia using oil. With the former, chirashi-zushi, there is something peaceful and 'Japanese' about the way in which the raw ingredients are layered. The dish does not depend on oil or heat, it highlights the main ingredient while creating a beautiful balance between it and the less important ones, and seems to express the Japanese mind. With the latter, although these dishes are cooked with oil, which is a technique imported from the Asian mainland, they can also be made in a Japanese way, for

Reclaiming the model of Japanese cuisine

example, by keeping the amount of oil used to a minimum, and arranging them in a neat, clean way. The 'Western learning' is not only Western-style cooking, but would have to include things that are influenced by Western philosophy. If not, they would be simple imitations. Accordingly, one needs to understand the significance of creativity within Western learning.

In this way, one can see the importance of the various elements that form the background to food, but I think our failure to understand this in more than a vague way might point to the roots of a weakness that can be sensed in modern Japan.

In actual fact, the examples given above do not provide a complete picture of Japanese food. For example, while we recognise that *ramen* originally came from China, this is something that we have been familiar with for a long time. The same is true for *gyōza* (Chinese dumplings filled with ground meat or vegetables) or *karé raisu* (gently spiced Japanese curry, typically prepared using a block of curry mix), although when these foods first arrived in Japan, they were not integrated into Japanese cuisine but treated as foreign food.

Although we do not think of ramen as belonging to Japanese cuisine in the strictest sense (in the discussions leading up to the UNESCO Intangible Cultural

Heritage registration, it was not considered to fall within the framework for Japanese food), the rest of the world considers it to be Japanese and it has become universally popular. Ramen is something that was developed in Japan by sheer ingenuity. Although Japanese society tends to be highly regulated, sometimes extraordinary things appear as sub-cultures in areas where there is no regulation. Here, young Japanese took something that was originally foreign, applied their inherently Japanese approach, and created something new.

The Japanese cuisine of the future might be born out of a synthesis involving this Japanese approach. But what ought to be borne in mind here is that great things are unlikely to result from random combinations. Simply putting wasabi and soy sauce on something does not make it Japanese cuisine, in the same way that cooking something in butter and adding a sauce does not make it French. I think what is important, if it is going to be genuine, is that it is taken in context and conforms to its essence.

It also seems worth noting that Japanese things that are globally successful are often created in areas where Japanese people are not constrained by any sense of hierarchy, as is the case with ramen or manga.

Cultural hierarchy has no place within our homes, so there is no reason for us to stick to Japanese cuisine. We can eat Western food, Chinese food or curry, or anything else we want. I think most Japanese people would find it hard to say that they regularly eat Japanese cuisine. But having acknowledged this problem, it is important for us to try to preserve it. When we adopt the realistic model of one soup and one side dish, which contains the essence of Japanese cuisine – that is, the idea that we should bring out the best in the raw ingredients we use – I think this becomes possible. By interpreting what it means for something to be 'Japanese' through the sustainable meal model that is one soup and one side dish, I believe that we can even pass it on to future generations.

The Pleasure That Begins with One Soup and One Side Dish

一汁一菜からはじまる楽しみ

Everyday pleasure

Imagine eating white rice and miso soup with lots of ingredients every day. Make sure you fill up your rice bowl properly. Doesn't that look nice? Just this is enough to make me happy; just looking at it makes me feel satisfied. People sometimes ask, 'What do you want to eat before you die?' and as you might have guessed, I think I would want freshly cooked rice with the option of seconds. If I could also have some silky miso soup and a side dish that goes well with rice (such as pickles), I think that would be enough. Come to think of it, that's what I eat every day.

Before you eat, you need to arrange your rice, miso soup and pickles attractively. Arranging these items into a neat triangle is a good starting point for enjoying your food. Put the rice on the left, the soup on the right, the pickles at the top, and your chopsticks in front of you. If you always do it like this, I think your children will develop good table manners and will

◗ Rice, Miso Soup, Pickles

learn how to eat Japanese food. You can teach them how to make what is in front of them look nice, and keep everything in order. I think even an adult might naturally sit up straighter if they have beautiful food in front of them. This is the beginning of food education.

The pleasure of choosing and using a rice bowl

Something that you touch and use every day should be something nice. Prioritise what you use on a daily basis rather than what is kept for special days, and take good care of it. It is not just people that refine their tools; the right tools can have a good effect on people too. In Japan and some parts of mainland Asia, every member of the family will often have their own rice bowl, teacup and chopsticks and, as a result, will feel a particular affection for the things that only they use.

What seems nice will differ from one person to another, so please choose things that everyone will like! I wrote that last sentence thinking about you shopping for your children, but do not put your own needs off until later – make sure you choose properly for yourself too. I remember when I was at primary school, my mother took me to Shinsaibashi in Osaka, home to one

Rice, Miso Soup, Pickles

of the busiest and oldest shopping streets in Japan, and let me choose my own rice bowl in a crockery shop there. I looked long and hard, and when I chose a very adult-looking *shonzui*-style teacup (blue and white porcelain decorated with geometric patterns) and a delicate porcelain rice bowl, she bought them for me, saying, 'You chose the best quality items in the whole shop.' In those days, rice bowls always came with a lid that you could turn upside down and use as a small dish.

Not all dishes are the same. A good dish will make even the most ordinary stir-fry look delicious. There are some bowls that feel good to touch and are easy to hold, and others that feel nice if you bring them up to your lips. Your rice bowl should also suit you! When you come to choose it, look at yourself holding it in the mirror, just as you would do when choosing clothes, and you will see that some suit you while others do not. I think something that reflects some aspect of your personality would be a good choice.

What do you think? I bet you want one now. But don't go out to buy it just yet. Wait for the right moment. Thinking about it and looking for it is enjoyable too. Fashion is fun, but do not let it seduce you; look at old things and plain things too. If you have the opportunity to visit a Japanese folk-art museum or a craft shop, you are bound to find something. I think

The pleasure of choosing and using a rice bowl

you are likely to find the right one when you are least thinking about it. Year by year, as you get older and your eye becomes more discerning, the things you like will start to change. If you pay attention to your changing tastes, you will get a sense of your personal growth. You may have thought you understood something a year ago, but in fact you didn't understand it at all. When you notice this, it's a sign that you have grown.

The rice bowl that was bought for me when I was a child was not given to me straight away. I had to wait until New Year, when new things are typically inaugurated, and I enjoyed looking forward to having it. However old we are, we never lose the pleasure we get from using something new.

Something you touch every day should be something nice – choose a bowl that you will enjoy using.

The pleasure when others notice your efforts, the pleasure of guessing what others have done

Through the invention of cooking, human beings rationalised the consumption of food (from finding and gathering food, chewing and swallowing it, digesting it and absorbing its energy, through to the excretion of waste products) and for the first time acquired extra time that was different from rest, in other words, leisure. Leisure is time when you are released from work, time that you can use as you wish. When people first had leisure, I wonder what they did with it? If the function of human life is love, I think they would probably have done something not for themselves, but for someone else.

The pleasure when others notice your efforts

Leisure means thinking of the smiling faces of one's family members, dressing up to go out. Carefully cleaning the house. Growing vegetables. Planting flowers. Travelling a long way to gather nuts or ripe fruits. It means doing things you do not have to do if you just want to survive, doing kindnesses for others, things for your own emotional well-being. In earlier times, nothing was done for remuneration, including many of the things we think of as work today, and so these leisure activities were probably done to bring pleasure to the family. I imagine people looked forward to bringing joy to others. In this sense, I wonder whether we, in modern times, still have the same kind of 'leisure' that our ancestors enjoyed? What does leisure mean for people today?

Busy with the daily grind, imagine that you continue to make one soup and one side dish. Every day, a soup and a side dish, the same every time. When you are busy, until you've accomplished some big project, there is no alternative, because you have no spare capacity to make anything special. The blessings of the seasons naturally bring changes throughout the year, but you barely have time to notice them.

You have given up on holidays, so it's the same at the weekend – one soup and one side dish. It has helped you lose weight, and since you started cooking

Rice, Miso Soup, Pickles

according to this model, you feel good. If you are someone who cooks for your family every day, your family will appreciate the fact that you no longer get so frustrated by the daily chores, but once one soup and one side dish becomes the norm, they will stop expecting anything else. Well, personally I don't think that's such a bad thing.

Then one day, imagine that you have finished up some work and are on the way home. You are in a good mood and so you pop into the supermarket. At the fish counter, you see they have some delicious-looking salmon. 'I fancy some of that,' you think to yourself, and with this type of fish, you can simply grill it while the miso soup is cooking. Everybody will be pleased, and when you think of your family's faces, you feel a little bit excited.

Later on, expecting nothing special, your family comes to the dinner table. Then, at the same time, they all gasp, 'Wow! There is fish today too!' Even without your saying anything, they all notice by themselves and feel glad (although I think they would probably have worked it out from the smell of fish grilling...).

It might seem obvious that they would notice something like this, but in fact it is not. Before you started cooking one soup and one side dish, you always

The pleasure when others notice your efforts

prepared something different every day, even if it took a lot of effort. Sometimes you would make something special, hoping to please your family, but nobody would notice. Eating a wide variety of dishes every day was something they had come to expect. Making so much effort had become normal for you too, and you probably thought, 'That's just how it is.'

If you have spare time and energy and see something that looks delicious when you are out shopping, and if you feel like eating it, you will probably think of your family (or whoever you normally cook for) too. This is because you want to make them happy – it is a very pure, natural thought. It is not a duty, or a job, or something someone else is forcing you to do. It is a very natural and pure reaction. If you cook when you feel like this, you will notice that it is not a big effort, but simply a pleasure. It is just the same as when you go to a nice restaurant for a work-related dinner, and decide to take your family there next time, or when you take someone on holiday because you want to show them a particular view that you like.

When I was a child and had to spend the evening alone at home, I would sometimes make dinner for my parents without telling them, and then wait impatiently for them to get home and notice. Before they came home, I would carefully clean and tidy my room, and then when they finally arrived, wait for their reaction. This wanting to be praised by the people we love, wanting to see the smiling faces of the people we really like, comes from love. The pure pleasure of cooking is not something that is forced, but bubbles up when there are no expectations. Cooking when it feels like this is something special. It is fine if it is not like this all the time. Our universal, beautiful food culture was born from a place of generosity, from a love that asked for nothing in return.

In the tea ceremony, the greatest pleasure for the host is when the guests notice and appreciate all the trouble she has gone to (not merely in serving the tea,

The pleasure when others notice your efforts

but choosing an appropriate kimono, practising the ceremony, purifying the utensils, preparing the space with seasonal flower arrangements, finding seasonal sweets to accompany the tea, etc.), without her having to say anything. This feeling of mutual understanding between the host and the guest is known as 'reciprocal hospitality'.

But this feeling is not limited to the tea ceremony. When you visit the house of an acquaintance, then obviously it is very nice if you notice the effort they have made, the flowers they have put in a vase, the delicious cakes and tea, and comment on these things straight away. Even if you make a mistake, your observations will still be appreciated. Your acquaintance will probably think what a lovely person you are, and that is the power of communication.

The pleasure of using a beautiful tray

If you eat by yourself often, then you might want to consider using a wooden tray or *ozen**. You can carry a tray anywhere in the house, and it makes tidying up afterwards more convenient. Wherever you place your tray, whether you are in Japan or abroad, that is your dining table.

---

* With a diameter of 30–45cm, this individual serving tray would traditionally have been made of black or red lacquered wood. The *bakozen* ('box tray'), consisting of a wooden box for tidying away your teacup, soup bowl, plate and chopsticks, fitted with a lid that could be turned upside down and used as a tray, was also popular. The *oshiki* is a kind of tray that is placed directly on tatami matting and is used in the tea ceremony. When furniture became Westernised, these trays were placed on tables. Ozen with feet were originally used as offerings to the gods.

The pleasure of using a beautiful tray

The reason that I would recommend using a tray is that the rim creates a distinction between the inside and outside of the (miniature) dining area and makes a natural barrier or boundary. Even if your desk is messy, the tray will be clean and tidy. As a result, there is a clear demarcation line around your meal and you will be able to give it your full attention. I think that by using a tray, you will be able to find pleasure in eating properly.

A wooden tray does not need to be washed if it is not especially dirty – you can just wipe it with a cloth. The more you do this, the more you will bring out the patterns in the wood, which is itself a pleasure: you will become more and more attached to it.

You can think of the tray as a kind of stage for your food, or a picture frame around your one soup and one side dish. A picture frame can be used only once, but a tray can be used again and again: it will always offer a new setting for your food. Every time you arrange your rice, miso soup and pickles on the tray, you renew the model and can take a new mental snapshot.

When we eat as a family, we do not use trays except on very special occasions. But in times gone by, people in Japan would have used a *chabudai*, a kind of low dining table that was reserved for meals and kept

Rice, Miso Soup, Pickles

tidied away at other times. At ordinary mealtimes, the chabudai would have been like a tray for the whole family. I think the reason I feel bad if I do not tidy the dining table before laying it for meals might come from this custom. If you are eating on your own, even if you don't tidy up your books and your work papers, you can use a tray and still eat properly. If you are eating as a family, you probably will not go as far as to use trays, but if you want to create a different mood, you could try using more formal place settings such as placemats.

The pleasure of sake, the pleasure of side dishes, the pleasure of the seasons (and enjoying what is in season)

Sake was originally only served on celebratory days. People would have a drink, put themselves in a bit of a good mood, and communicate with the gods. Today, we still drink sake for pleasure. When you serve sake, you should add another seasonal delicacy to your menu. Then, one soup and one side dish will become one soup and two side dishes. If you have fruit as well, that will make three.

Even in modern times, despite increasing urbanisation and the resulting decrease in green spaces, our enjoyment of the seasons in home cooking remains unchanged. Japanese sensitivity has been honed by this awareness of the changing of the seasons, so I think it is worth preserving. In Japan, the four seasons are further subdivided into twenty-four 'solar terms', which gives one an idea of this sensitivity. At this point in the book, I would like to mention a few raw and cooked dishes that might go well with sake, to accompany the twenty-four solar terms. Even if they do not go so well with rice, I think you will enjoy them, so I have tried to set them down as they occurred to me.

The pleasures of spring

When we think of the start of spring in Japan, we usually think of the New Year, but according to the twenty-four solar terms, spring starts on the day following *setsubun* (literally, 'seasonal division'), which is usually celebrated between the 2nd and 4th February and continues as far as the day before *rikka* (literally, 'the start of summer'), celebrated on the 5th or 6th May. And indeed, the time of year when the blossoms start to open feels very springlike indeed.

Spring is the season of bitter tastes. If you find *fukinotō* (the edible flower buds of the *Petasites japonicus* plant, an early spring delicacy), you can cut them finely, pound and mix them together with miso and sugar to make fukinotō miso. If you can obtain young burdock root, and carefully clean the young green stems, these can be sautéed. These young plants definitely herald spring.

Spring is also the time of buds. Water dropwort that grows where cold spring water flows from melting snow, served *ohitashi*-style, blanched and steeped in a dashi-based sauce or in a *shiraae* salad with mashed tofu, white sesame and white miso. Spring onions grown beneath the snow, served with a *karashi-su-miso* (mustard miso) dressing. Field horsetail, boiled and served in an egg soup. Clams steamed with sake.

From about mid-March, the Japanese pepper plant at my house begins to bud. In the Kansai area where I live, we call these buds *kinome* ('tree buds'). They go well with bamboo shoots and fried meat. The fragrance of kinome really makes me feel like spring. Then there is *sukiyaki* (a hot pot made with meat and vegetables, simmered in a broth of soy sauce, sugar and mirin) with *sansai* (edible wild plants). If you quickly boil new bamboo shoots, steep them in iced water and then keep them in the fridge, you can serve them in various different ways, for example, boiled, fried in soy sauce or with olive oil and mayonnaise, or as *tempura* (coated in a thin batter and deep fried). I use Japanese yam in miso soup made with tinned mackerel. I also like to eat lightly boiled giant butterbur.

In April, the temperatures start to rise and it gets a bit more springlike: there is more light, and peas and beans begin to flourish. I like to shell fresh green peas and steam them mixed in with my rice.

Spring is also the season for shellfish. Shellfish are available at the supermarket almost all year round, but they have the deepest umami flavour and are at their most delicious as they approach the spawning season, that is, in February and March.

The period from April through to May and June is the season for fishing from the rocks by the seashore. Fish that taste good when boiled down in soy sauce, such as black rock fish, sillago or summer grunt, are also good when deep fried.

The pleasures of summer

Summer is generally thought to be the period from rikka in May to the day before *risshū* ('the start of summer') on the 7th or 8th August. While May tends

The pleasure of sake, the pleasure of side dishes

to feel like a continuation of spring, once I can feel the intensity of the sun's rays, I know that summer has started. Foods that are seasonal for May include beans and bamboo shoots, things that 'face the heavens', and May must the best season for all kinds of beans, since they are called *satsukimame* ('May beans'). I think they feel delicious when you touch them – choose the ones that are nice and soft. At around the same time, summery new onions and new potatoes will appear. New onions are delicious if you just slice them finely: I like to eat them with a little vinegar.

Water shield is only available in this season. You can boil it and make a quick pickle. From about mid-June, the true summer vegetables start to appear. When it gets to this time of year, I always want to eat *ayu* (sweetfish) but depending on the conditions in any given year, this is not always possible.

For *yakınasu* (grilled aubergine), it is best if you can grill it until the skin is charred – even the parts where the skin peels should be slightly burnt – the aroma is quite different. Put any leftovers in the fridge: I recommend eating them with grated ginger and soy sauce. Sometimes you can also get small, soft bell peppers and shishito peppers at this time of year, and you can fry these whole in oil or simmer them *netsuke*-style with sake, mirin and soy sauce.

Rice, Miso Soup, Pickles

When summer vegetables are good, they will automatically make good *nukazuke* (pickles made with brine and fermented rice bran). In the summer, I can eat these every day without tiring of them and sometimes they can be a meal in themselves. If you have any old pickles that taste a bit vinegary, then you can chop them into small pieces, rinse them in cold water and serve them with grated ginger. Whenever I get out the aubergine pickles that I order especially from Osaka, people are really pleased, so I try to make sure I have some all year round.

Summer is the season for sour tastes, for example, *sunomono* ('vinegared things') made with cucumber that has been briefly steeped in salt and then rinsed in cold water, wakame and dried young sardines. Octopus with vinegared miso. Small horse mackerel fried with spring onions and chilli. You can make quick pickles with Japanese rice vinegar. The summer mood continues until around *obon* (a festival to honour the deceased, which lasts several days and is usually celebrated in mid-August).

The pleasures of autumn

Autumn is the period from risshū in August to the day before *rittō* ('the start of winter') on around the 7th or 8th November. Among the first pleasures of autumn are the new mackerel pike that appear at the end of summer. When I have them grilled with salt, I feel as if I could eat them every day. Accompanied by plenty of grated daikon radish, they make me feel blessed. Having said that, I do eventually get bored, and instead simmer them in vinegar and soy sauce until they are quite soft to make *karani*. I think things with a mature flavour and things that are thickly sliced seem more delicious in autumn.

In September, there are new chestnuts. If you find any, you can stew them thoroughly in their skins, halve them, and then eat them with a spoon. You can also scoop out the flesh from stewed chestnuts, add some salt and boil them down with sake to make chestnut *tsubuan* (sweet chestnut paste). This will not make a side dish, but instead of serving the tsubuan with rice flour dumplings, you can add them to rice to make *ohagi* (sweet rice balls coated in tsubuan). You can make golden yellow *imoan* (sweet potato paste) by mashing sweet potatoes with gardenias until they are soft and then flavouring them with butter and sugar. I have this with my toast in the morning, but it does not work as an appetiser for sake.

Miso soup with plenty of mushrooms and chicken makes an autumnal miso soup. The taste of *maitake* (hen-of-the-woods) mushrooms simmered in soy sauce with beef offcuts is just as good as meat. These days, unfortunately, I barely ever eat matsutake mushrooms. If I can get hold of large shiitake mushrooms, I fry them in butter and eat them with *sudachi* (a small green citrus fruit with a tart, acidic taste) and soy sauce. If you boil taro in its skin, it broadens the scope of your cooking. It is good if you just mash it, sprinkle it with flour and then fry it in oil on both sides, but you can also use it to make *agedashi* with mashed taro (dusting it with potato starch, deep frying it and coating it in a savoury sauce) or mash it and add it to miso soup.

If you find salted salmon roe, then it is surprisingly easy to prepare *ikura* (salmon caviar) and you can enjoy a feeling of luxury. It is excellent with new rice.

Around the time when the gingko nuts fall and the leaves start to turn, the temperature starts to drop and it finally feels like autumn. If I find some really ripe gingko nuts, I hit them with a hammer one by one so that they split and then fry them in an earthenware pan. It makes a snack that is not only delicious but very healthy too.

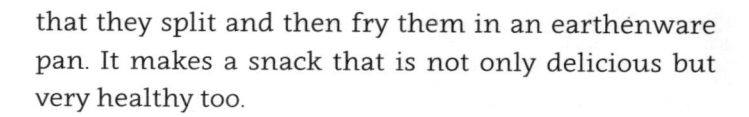

The pleasures of winter

Winter is the time from rittō to setsubun in February. The main pleasures of winter are things that give warmth. If you take some tofu, boil it and eat it with freshly mixed *tsukeshōyū* (soy sauce, mirin and sake), it's exceptional. I also put tofu, *konnyaku* (a jelly made from the starchy tuber of the konjac plant) and sweet potato on skewers to make *dengaku* (grilling and glazing the skewers with a sweet and savoury miso sauce), and recently I have been putting plenty of grated ginger in my glaze. Sea cucumber is surprisingly cheap, so I cut thick slices of that and eat it with vinegar and soy sauce mixed in roughly equal proportions.

At my house, summer pickles give way to pickled Chinese cabbage in the winter. We make enough pickled Chinese cabbage to last until the following spring. It starts to taste delicious after around 2–3 weeks, when it begins to have a slightly sour taste, and I can eat it every day without getting bored. The large,

Rice, Miso Soup, Pickles

leafy Chinese cabbages that are found towards the end of the year make the best pickles.

Daikon is available all year round, but the daikon that you can get in December is truly delicious. If you cook it with just dashi broth and deep-fried tofu, you can make *daikondaki*. This is good served both hot and cold.

Before you know it, it is the end of the year. In December, in Japan, we all pound mochi rice to make seasonal rice mochi and prepare for the New Year. As you might expect, mochi rice pounded with a mallet tastes different. The chief pleasure of the New Year is osechi ryōri. In our house, it is my wife who carefully chooses the raw ingredients and prepares all our New Year's dishes. Then, on the seventh breakfast of the year, we have *nanagusagayu* ('seven herb rice porridge'), but it is so delicious that we make it on other days too.

When the New Year begins and it gets very cold, the delicious flavours of spinach and *komatsuna* (Japanese mustard spinach) really come into their own. If you simmer komatsuna with deep-fried tofu it will melt in your mouth. Spinach has such nice red roots, and in winter I often use it to make ohitashi. I fry *kezurikatsuo* (dried bonito shavings) and then put this on top.

Cabbage was also originally a winter vegetable and this is why domestically grown Brussels sprouts are only available at this time of year. If you deep-fry Brussels sprouts without any batter, the inner surfaces of the outside leaves taste as if they had been steamed and then fried. I recommend enjoying them with a little salt.

Winter is the season for big fish like Japanese amberjack. This is very good cooked *teriyaki*-style (broiled or grilled with a glaze of soy sauce, mirin and sugar) or with daikon.

In this section, I have set out a few dishes that work both as an appetiser with sake and as a side dish for rice and miso soup. Using the same ingredients and the same recipes, you can make either the appetiser or the side dish, as the mood takes you. If you are making them to go with rice, then you should aim for a deeper flavour; when making appetisers, a lighter flavour will suffice.

I always think it is nice to say something apt when serving seasonal dishes. 'Look, the first cherries!' 'Skipjack tuna is good this year, isn't it!' 'The bitterness of these butterbur buds is good for you!' 'These tomatoes and aubergines are from grandma's allotment!' 'Things in season are so delicious' 'We haven't had any bamboo shoots yet this year!' 'You should finish it or it'll go to waste!' 'This is the last of the Chinese cabbage pickles, no more until next year!' You too may find yourself saying something like this, every time you make them, every year.

Enjoying Japanese food culture and the pleasure of beauty

Once you have made a few different dishes, you will achieve a certain balance across the table (or tray) as a whole. You can create a single menu, taking into account the actual colours, textures, quantities and other aspects of the different dishes. With cooking, the taste of a particular dish can seem very different depending on whether you eat it on its own or alongside a few other dishes. If you do prepare various different dishes to be eaten together, somehow there will always be a main character and a supporting cast. Once you have decided on the main one, the trick is to make sure the others don't steal the show. If you manage this, then sometimes the other dishes will taste even nicer than you expected. When preparing this type of dish, you can sometimes halve the amount of seasoning given in the recipe and sometimes leave it out altogether. Once you have understood this type of thing, I think you are well on your way to understanding Japanese cooking.

Anyway, as I said earlier, one of the important factors behind 'eating with your eyes' and enjoying texture in Japanese cuisine is the plates, bowls and dishes it is served in. Just like flavouring, the appearance of the dishes will depend on whether you see them one at a time or in combination with others. Beauty depends on balance, whether you are selecting your shirt and tie for the day or laying the table. People with good taste are cool, and this has nothing to do with the price of their clothes. With dishes, it depends on what combination of porcelain, pottery, earthenware and lacquer you use. It is hard to explain it in just a few words, and I will leave that for another occasion, but for example, if you arrange a sake bottle, a sake cup and a small bowl or plate on a tray, enjoy this first, and then bring out a whole new tray with one soup and one side dish. It can look completely different and feel really nice. This is known as *ozenkae* ('a change of tray') and can add a touch of luxury to your everyday soup and side dish – if you have guests, then I am sure they will enjoy it too.

In this way, by virtue of its very simplicity, one soup and one side dish gives you the chance to be creative. You don't need to ask an expert. We seem to be living in the age of the expert: if you are not an expert in something, you cannot do it or even talk about it. But lovely things can and may be made by anyone at all. Lovely things are everywhere – we are surrounded by them in our daily lives. The truly beautiful things, the things that the sacred spirits reveal to us, are unique, but if you are looking for something that fits onto the palm of your hand, you will not have to look very far. Follow your instincts when you find yourself thinking 'That's beautiful, that's good.'

One soup and one side dish is the starting point for understanding Japanese food culture.

Taking the everyday food in one soup and one side dish as the basis, you can enjoy sake with a seasonal appetiser, prepare the best possible meal that you can and, at the end, enjoy a cup of tea: this is just like a tea ceremony.

If you prefer to enjoy your sake without a soup and a side dish, you can still put a seasonal appetiser on an attractive dish and enjoy it, even if you are on your own. You could even use something you consider inappropriate for a proper meal, for example, something you might think of as a work of art. One soup and one side dish is a single idea that connects everything from everyday cooking to the art of the tea ceremony.

Rice, Miso Soup, Pickles

Please adopt one soup and one side dish – recipes from Japanese cuisine – as part of your everyday home cooking. Anyone can make rice, miso soup and pickles. If you arrange everything neatly and live humbly, you will develop a new sensitivity and be full of peace. Please make seasonal dishes on days when you have time to spare. You probably already know about the joy of cooking and seeing the smiling faces of the people eating. Please invite guests sometimes, too. Prepare some tasty titbits, choose some pretty plates, and pile everything up. Create a space to enjoy reciprocal hospitality. By doing so, you will preserve Japanese food culture, and pass it on to your children and the generations to come.

One soup and one side dish on a tray: everyday pleasures. Rice, miso soup and grilled fish with two vegetable dishes.

Japanese people who live beautifully – in lieu of a conclusion

Among my friends there is one who comes with me when I gather edible plants and mushrooms. He decided he preferred being in the countryside, so he quit his job as a businessman and works in the mountains now, where he grows rice, chestnuts and vegetables. His name is Yoshio Horigome. He is 10 years older than me, but he is lean, tall, youthful and stylish.

During the rainy season at the start of summer, his wife joined us for a walk in the mountains. Due to the altitude, we were surrounded by plants that were still a pale shade of green, and, walking through the misty rain, the cool and humid air felt refreshing. My friend pointed out the faint sound of water, which was

Rice, Miso Soup, Pickles

mixed with the chirping of the birds and the sound of the wind rustling the leaves, and which was coming from somewhere below his right hand. He seemed to be keenly interested in the sound of this water flowing in a river somewhere – more interested than I would have expected – and started to tell me where the water had collected, and where it had flowed from, quite as if he had seen it with his own eyes under the ground. 'It's going from that mountain over there to this stream over here. Look how big the leaves of this bamboo grass are, and opposite there's that big tree . . .' I had absolutely no idea what he was talking about. Just then his wife, who was with us, said, 'We get it. Give it a rest!' 'Once he starts talking about that stuff, there's no stopping him,' she added.

I am sure she was just trying to be considerate towards me, but I don't know anyone else who will hear the sound of water running in the mountains and then tell you under which tree roots and under which rocks it is flowing, and I thought it was amazing. I was impressed by this new side of my friend.

I don't think it's right to call someone 'primitive' or 'wild' if they have this type of skill. 'Wild' describes someone with a rough nature who cannot control their instincts. By contrast, my friend has a peaceful nature, and the kind of understanding inherent in

Japanese people who live beautifully – in lieu of a conclusion

genuine people. I think modern people often use the idea of 'understanding' with respect to culture, but I think in my friend's case, it was human reason responding to nature, which is larger and greater than man. It was his innate intelligence sensing something important about water as a continuation of life.

A little later, we were walking along a path with tall bamboo plants on both sides, when Horigome-san suddenly stopped by some bamboo leaves that, to me, seemed indistinguishable from all the others, and disappeared into the bamboo grove. I was just starting to think he'd vanished, when he emerged from the thicket carrying a large bamboo shoot in his arms. Bamboo shoots grow at a 50- or 60-degree angle to the ground, spreading out and crossing each other in a complex network to the left and right, and this can make it very hard for people to move around. In a bamboo thicket, you can really only move by going under and over the plants or trampling them down. These thickets tend to be dense, so that once someone enters them, even if they are just a few metres away, you will no longer see them even if you can still hear their voice.

However, Horigome-san could move as quickly as a monkey inside a thicket like this. When I indicated my surprise, he said, 'Bears are much faster. Once

Rice, Miso Soup, Pickles

they can push their thin noses in, they smash their way through with brute force.' Well, although bears are a very real danger in Japan, I knew I was safe with Horigome-san. He could shimmy up a tree and survey the lie of the land, memorising the shapes and sizes of several trees that could serve as way-markers at a single glance, but I would not have dreamed of going into the thicket by myself. The three of us (mainly Horigome-san, actually) then spent a little while digging up another enormous bamboo shoot that I could only just carry with both hands.

When we got back to Horigome-san's house, we set about cleaning the bamboo shoots we had found. When you are gathering wild plants, however many you gather, you need to deal with them on the same day. As far as Horigome-san is concerned, gathering wild plants does not mean going for a lovely walk and picking a bit of young bracken or some giant butterbur if you happen to spot it. For him, it was a case of deciding on a particular plant at the appropriate time: if you were looking for flowering fern, you would gather flowering fern. When I look at Horigome-san, I can't help thinking that's what a foraging lifestyle has always been about.

Next, we spread out a straw mat on the floor and set about peeling the bamboo shoots. He had a tool

Japanese people who live beautifully – in lieu of a conclusion

consisting of a ring with metal teeth around the inside, and if a thin bamboo shoot was pushed through it, it would come out covered in neat incisions. Once all of them had been covered in incisions, it was time to peel them. The incisions went from the tip to the base of the shoot, so the idea was to hold the base and peel the skin in sections towards the tip. If it went well, you should be able to peel each section cleanly and end up with something that looked a bit like a freshly sharpened pencil. I had no idea that a freshly dug, freshly peeled bamboo shoot was such a vivid shade of green.

If we did not manage to peel the bamboo shoots, we would not be able to eat them, so we all got down to work. I had set out to go for a walk in the mountains, ended up going into a bamboo thicket, and, having found the last bamboo shoots of the year, had my first experience of gathering bamboo shoots. I only realised when we were talking about it afterwards, but when I thought I had been digging up bamboo shoots I was actually breaking them.

As soon as I had been shown the correct technique and was starting to understand the basics, I wanted to know how I could get a clean peel as quickly as possible. Using my chef's knowledge and experience, I tried to think of the most logical way to peel the bamboo shoots, and my hands got to work. Obviously it wasn't a competition or anything, but in situations like this I always concentrate on trying to get the first prize. But just when I thought I had got it, I realised that the size and softness of every bamboo shoot is different. Every time I thought I had got the hang of it, I would let my guard down and damage one, and every time I damaged one, I regretted it.

I stopped for a moment and looked over at Horigome-san and was struck by the beauty of his hands. For me, beautiful hands are hands you might see when a group of older women in the countryside have gathered at a pool by the edge of a river and are washing the greens they have just harvested in their fields. I couldn't help staring – when I think of 'good hands' now, it's his that I think of.

Those good hands picked up the bamboo shoots he had peeled one by one and stacked them into a pyramid. It seemed amazing that none of them were damaged. Horigome-san was not thinking about being faster than the rest of us, having a competition, looking cool, how to peel them logically or politely or anything like that. In other words, he had absolutely none of the idle thoughts that were going around my mind. However good I got, I think I would always end up damaging a few.

Japanese people who live beautifully – in lieu of a conclusion

I have admired good hands, and people who have them, for a long time, and I felt that on that day, I understood for the first time what it meant to have good hands. I trusted and believed in those hands absolutely. And I realise that it may be impossible, but I still think I would like to have good hands one day too. Young people still have time. If they are careful, they can have any kind of hands they like. And I'm not talking about dexterity and clumsiness, being good or not good at things. There's more to it than that.

Rice, Miso Soup, Pickles. I was just wondering what it was that I really wanted to say with this book. I wanted to say, rice, miso soup and pickles are *enough*, this is all you need, but in the course of explaining why they were enough, I ended up having to explain the wisdom contained in Japanese culture and how it came to be this way.

Ultimately, this is bound up with the relationship between man and nature or otentosama, the 'omnipresent sun', that is to say, a way of thinking about things that I think the Japanese have probably managed to preserve in its purest form from ancient times. It is also connected to things that great writers have already explained elsewhere, to what Norinaga Motoori calls the 'ancient Japanese spirit', and without really meaning to, I ended up touching on some rather ambitious topics. I am still feeling a little perplexed about this, and I would welcome any criticisms or comments that you may have.

But getting back to those 'good hands'.

Minoru Kumoda, that master of miso soup who passed away in 2014, was a true role model for me. He was also someone who came into the mountains with me, gathering edible wild plants in spring and mushrooms in autumn. In order that I could take them back to Tokyo with me, he would clean the various wild mushrooms, sandwich them in between the leaves of trees to prevent them drying out and turn the whole thing into a little box. I was always captivated by the beauty of these little gifts. However often I stood next to him and copied him as he folded the leaves, what his hands managed to produce was on a different level to my clumsy efforts. He even made beautiful little bundles from the sticks he cut to make chopsticks, wrapping each one in a butterbur leaf he found nearby. When he got thirsty, he would find one of the mountain springs that are so numerous in summer, roll up a butterbur leaf and make a cup to drink from.

Japanese people who live beautifully – in lieu of a conclusion

The miso soup that he made was sometimes judged to be the best in Japan. He became very well-known, and researchers from major food manufacturers would travel incognito to visit him and learn about the subtle changes in flavour that do not show up in measurements or statistics. I realised what a truly rare person he was when I saw the magnificence of his garden. Plants from different altitudes, plants that like water, plants that hate water and plants from completely different habitats were all sitting on the same shelf, happily flowering and fruiting side by side. It was a bonsai collection consisting mainly of wild grasses and flowers that he had spent more than 50 years putting together. When he invited me to a lecture of the Waseda University Food Culture Research Group, I was surprised to hear him say that he had no recollection of any plants ever dying. One of his favourite phrases was, 'Good sake and good miso are not made by people – anyone conceited enough to say they made them should be strictly admonished.' Well, we all believed what he said about his plants.

The graphic designer Ikko Tanaka, while he was still alive, used to cook for his staff whenever he was in the studio. He loved both cooking and eating, and I think I must have been invited to at least twelve tea ceremonies where he had personally prepared the food. Although he left behind such a wonderful body of work, I heard from his niece, Chie (also a designer), that he used to say it would have been better if he had become a chef.

I recently found a DVD containing an interview with him, and in it he says, 'I love gardening. In the US they say someone has "green thumbs", don't they? I only need to show them a bit of love, and most plants get better. Even if I have a plant that looks like it is dying, if I snip off the buds and replant it, it will bud again and grow. There are people who say they can't do this, but I think it's all in the way you look at things. Just by looking at them, I know instinctively what they want me to do.' He was talking about the same thing as Kumoda-san.

There is another person whom I feel I have to mention here, someone very important to me. That is Noriko Hakozaki from the pottery shop, Yakimono Ikoma, which used to be in Ikoma in Nara. Whenever time allowed, I used to be in that shop. I would spend time with her, have a meal, drink tea, listen to her stories and look at the pottery that was arranged in great quantities but with great care on her shelves.

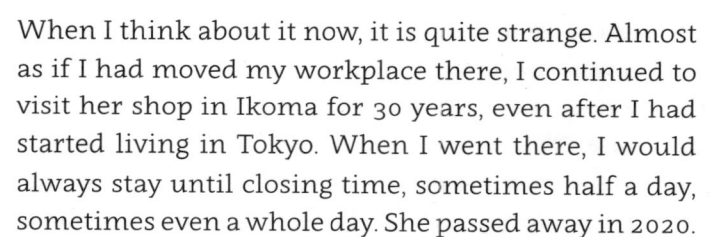

Japanese people who live beautifully – in lieu of a conclusion

When I think about it now, it is quite strange. Almost as if I had moved my workplace there, I continued to visit her shop in Ikoma for 30 years, even after I had started living in Tokyo. When I went there, I would always stay until closing time, sometimes half a day, sometimes even a whole day. She passed away in 2020.

The items in her shop were all things that she had selected and bought herself, visiting each maker in person on the one day each week when her shop was closed, and making day trips from Tokyo as far as Hokkaido in the very north of Japan, and Okinawa in the very south. Items for as little as a hundred yen rubbed shoulders with items that sold for as much as several million yen, jostling for a place on her crowded shelves. The shop was always full of customers, very young and very old, long-established chefs, connoisseurs of rare items, even people in the same trade – the things they all wanted were in Yakimono Ikoma.

When it got to lunchtime, Hakozaki-san would go upstairs to her kitchen and quickly make us some food. Every time I ate what she had prepared I wondered how she made it taste so delicious, and felt truly humbled.

One day, we were sitting in front of our food, and she realised that for some reason she had not given

Rice, Miso Soup, Pickles

me any chopsticks. She started searching high and low, and eventually pulled out some of those disposable chopsticks that come with a box of sushi from the back of a drawer – goodness knows how long they had been there. Muttering, 'This won't do at all,' Hakozaki-san held the chopsticks over the steam from the iron kettle for a little while, and then, apparently pleased with the results, placed them on my tray. As if she had performed some kind of magic, this humble thing seemed to have been changed into the most superior pair of chopsticks ever. This is the kind of person she was.

If it had not been for this shop, I think I would not have turned into the person I am today. There were pots of flowers at the front and at the back of the shop. Hakozaki-san would water them with a watering can every morning and every evening. There was a pot full of water lilies, with killifish that bred every year, and on summer mornings the lilies would open as if trying to stand up out of the water. The water was always clean and clear: there were marsh snails that ate the blue algae that built up inside the pot, and their young would in turn be eaten by the killifish – it was its own tiny ecosystem. When guests brought flowers, whether from their own garden or from a shop, it was as if they were

Japanese people who live beautifully – in lieu of a conclusion

happy just to be there, and flowered more beautifully there than anywhere else.

When Hakozaki-san made site visits to buy pottery, people paid attention to what she bought: there were even people who followed her around. Anything she so much as looked at or touched would always sell. By buying in works by young potters and drawing attention to the good aspects of their work, she helped a great many artists to become established. Artists cared so much about her judgement that it was more important for their work to be displayed in Yakimono Ikoma than to have a solo exhibition at a famous department store. I have to wonder at all the things I learnt by going there. It was a good shop that was loved by all, but the way she was able to quit so decisively at the end was particularly brilliant.

I think 'living beautifully' can be achieved through the relationship between people and nature. As we go about our daily lives, we bring our experience to bear on situations, wondering how to judge them, often struggling, and sometimes we do well and sometimes we make mistakes. But if we always strive to do our best, then I think the people that we meet while doing so will show us the way. I do not have the special abilities of any of the people I have just mentioned, but I think I have nevertheless managed to feel this through my cooking. I might wonder why something has turned out tasting delicious and something else has not, or wonder about things I cannot explain, and then one day it will suddenly become clear to me.

I do not think being able to produce delicious food is a skill. I also do not think someone will be able to make delicious things just because they have had many years of experience. The things an ordinary person cooks will often include particularly delicious things. Sometimes, dishes you have not put any special effort into will turn out tasting nicer than the most expensive cuisine. Some things are so beautiful that they cannot be expressed in monetary terms.

In Japanese culture, there is no insurmountable wall separating nature and man. This is why something similar to the spirit of the Jōmon people who lived in Japan long ago has survived. On these solitary islands, nature and man are somehow still in balance, as they always have been. As a consequence, we are now able to bring together the old, the not-so-old and the new, and bring out the best in all of them.

Japanese people who live beautifully – in lieu of a conclusion

To cook is to live. Today, just as in ancient times, I believe that cooking brings us into direct contact with nature.

The person who kindly created the cover design for this book was Taku Satō. Taku-san is very interested in the Jōmon period and asked Tatsuo Kobayashi, the leading expert in Jōmon studies, to teach him about it. Following this, he submitted a proposal to the National Science Museum, put on an exhibition about the people of the Jōmon period there, and went on to produce a beautiful book about the Jōmon mind called *Jomonese* (Bijutsu Shuppansha, 2012). I think Taku-san is someone who always thinks of the true nature of things. Thanks to his efforts, I was able to have dinner with Kobayashi-sensei, whom I had been wanting to meet for a long time. I was very excited to be able to talk about the Jōmon period with him.

Up until now, I have not dared to share the photograph of the 'miso soup made for purely personal consumption' (see page 67) with anyone else – this is from a series of genuine photographs that I took for my own use, showing the soup exactly as it was. These were all soups that I simply made, without even

Rice, Miso Soup, Pickles

tasting them. Miso is a natural product, so however you make miso soup, it is delicious. It might not be the kind of taste that will knock your socks off, but it will be delicious in its own way. I think this is the way it was made long ago, before people made any distinction between food that was delicious and food that was not.

Taku-san happened to look at the words 'the proposal that one soup and one side dish is enough' that I had scribbled in pencil, and without hesitating, added his design to them. Now to me, they do not look like they have been 'designed' at all, they still seem to be in that natural state before the arrival of the concept of design. Ikko Tanaka said, 'When you choose not to design something, that is still a design,' but you still need something to work with. Anyway, in order to turn my messy writing into something we could use on the cover, we decided to make the paper the colour of rice, the writing the colour of leaves, and the lower half of the page the colour of miso soup, and then carefully adjusted everything to achieve the right balance. The result is the cover of the Japanese edition. Incidentally, I was told that the colour of the brown band is taken from a photograph that Taku-san took of the miso soup he had for breakfast that morning. I was impressed by his wonderful design,

Japanese people who live beautifully – in lieu of a conclusion

which far exceeded my expectations. I would like to express my thanks for this again here.

My sincere thanks are also due to my wife, whose home cooked meals, prepared with such care, are a source of daily pleasure, and Kumi Ōba of Graphicsha, who became part of the team and supported me throughout.

And finally...

In the middle of your busy life, when you are giving it your all, there will probably be some days that are less good than others. Sometimes you will work hard, then stop to rest, and just as you start to relax, you catch a cold. The soup and the side dish for days when your body is sending out distress calls is okayu with miso and umeboshi. Cooking that you take your time over is kinder to your body when you are ill.

To make two bowls of okayu, wash half a cup of rice (you can also use araigome), put it in your saucepan, add six to seven times the volume of water and leave it to stand for 10 minutes. Then turn the heat up to a high setting. Once it has boiled, stir the rice to loosen it, move the lid to one side of the saucepan so as to leave a slight gap, and cook it on a low heat. The heat

Rice, Miso Soup, Pickles

should be just enough for the rice to simmer quietly. Peep in through the gap from time to time, adjusting the heat if necessary. For a healthy adult, you will need to let the rice simmer for just 20–30 minutes, but for a child, an elderly person or for yourself, if you are sick, you can leave it for longer: 40–50 minutes or even an hour or more is fine. If you are planning to simmer it for a long time, add a little more water at the beginning and use a very low heat setting. You can also feed this to a baby, but let the water evaporate fully and allow it to cool down first.

I very much hope that this book will benefit you, dear reader, as well as your children.

For my mother and father, who created the kitchen of all my experiences.

September 2016
Yoshiharu Doi

The future of one soup and one side dish – on the occasion of the paperback publication

It was the autumn of 2016, and *Ichijū Issai de Yoi to iu Teian* ('The Proposal That One Soup and One Side Dish Is Enough') had just been published. Tokyo, in that time before Covid, was said to be the best city in the world in which to enjoy gourmet food. Exclusive restaurants using luxury produce that was pushed onto a new generation of owners by young artisans and young chefs, proliferated. The city was in the middle of a gourmet boom.

The proposal to eat one soup and one side dish came right at this time. Moreover, it came from a food researcher who was associated with good food but who was also prone to saying things like, 'You don't

Rice, Miso Soup, Pickles

need to cook,' and 'Home cooking doesn't have to be delicious every day.' How would the public respond? I was actually quite worried that it would have a negative effect on my future work! But I resigned myself to this, since, as a food researcher, what I really want is for people to enjoy cooking.

However, as soon as the book was published, reader responses started to appear on social media, and they exceeded my hopes. 'I feel so much better.' 'I feel as if I have been released from eternal suffering.' 'I have changed the way I live.' 'One soup and one side dish saved my life.' 'I remembered why I used to like cooking.' 'I feel healthier.' 'I've lost weight.' 'This book changed my life.'

So, it was a helpful book after all. Someone told me there was no need to read what was inside, the title said it all. They did have a point there, I thought.

A caregiver told me that when she was cooking at the homes of her clients, she always struggled to think of what to prepare as a vegetable dish. She thanked me, saying, 'You taught me that I can put any vegetables I want into the miso soup.' When I was walking down the street, young women would often run after me, thanking me and saying how much the book had helped them. Veterans of the kitchen, women who had been preparing home-cooked meals all their

The future of one soup and one side dish

lives, told me, 'I feel like the things I have been doing all these years have finally been acknowledged, and that makes me happy,' and that made *me* feel happy too. It seemed as if mothers had not had the opportunity to be praised up until now.

There seemed to be so many women who were struggling every day with the burden of home cooking, it made me wonder how many people there were out there, suffering under a stress that had become normalised. If you look at the reader reviews, you will see what I mean.

At around this time, the brilliant art writer Mari Hashimoto, whom I hold in very high regard, was kind enough to write a wonderful review of the book in a newspaper. I have taken the liberty of setting it out below:

> The subject of cooking, which has become a universal indicator used for measuring not only degrees of affection and nutritional knowledge but even attitudes to life, has become a source of pressure for many, particularly women. There is now a way to disentangle oneself from this self-imposed trap: this book.
>
> Starting from the basis that you can cook rice and miso soup with lots of ingredients in just 20 minutes,

Rice, Miso Soup, Pickles

you will be surprised and delighted by the way in which this model lets you add seasonal variation to your cooking. The issue [of what to cook every day] is not just something for mothers and wives to worry about – it is for people at every stage of life, whether they have their meals cooked for them, cook their meals themselves or cook for others, and for people of any age, both men and women: given the necessity of cooking in order to eat and live, just doing it is enough of a task.

Shinano Mainichi Newspaper
(morning edition), 30 July 2017

I was told, 'Until I discovered the concept of one soup and one side dish, I had no confidence in my cooking,' 'I want to make and eat tasty things – please tell me how to make delicious things quickly!'

Writing 'The Proposal That One Soup and One Side Dish Is Enough' made me think more deeply about home cooking. I shouldn't have to go as far as to say 'home cooking', it should be enough to call it 'cooking', but these days when people say 'cooking', images of professional chefs and their creations mysteriously come to mind, so I use 'home cooking' to distinguish it from that done by professionals. Below I will just call it 'cooking'. Japanese cooking is designed to bring out

The future of one soup and one side dish

the best in the raw ingredients used. One of the ideals of washoku is therefore to do nothing, to leave shape and colour as they are, if possible, not even adding flavour. The style of eating that I refer to as 'one soup and one side dish' is a product of the indigenous beliefs in nature born out of a life of co-existence with, and dependence on, the rich natural environment of these solitary islands in East Asia and a diet connected to, and nurtured by, rice cultivation that came over the ocean from the Asian mainland. For this reason, the original form or concept still survives in Japanese cooking today. Although today, the original spirit of Japanese cuisine has perhaps been overlaid with the culture and ideas of Western cooking, and it has become difficult to make out, I believe that it is still there.

I think this type of cooking, which is connected to the natural environment from which it was born, still exists in other parts of the world too, but in Japan's case, it has deepened over time, and has even been elevated to an aesthetic ideal. Japan has one of the most diverse craft cultures in the world. The folk-art theory of Muneyoshi Yanagi is worth noting again at this point. The tea ceremony also grew out of an extremely pure kind of cooking, which can be connected to nature by a straight line: a philosophy

Rice, Miso Soup, Pickles

emerged to accompany the universal aesthetic and became an art.

I believe that cooking is a kind of philosophy.

In order to confirm this idea and in an attempt to broaden and deepen my thinking, I approached the following people:

- Hiroshi Shimizu, Doctor of Pharmaceutical Sciences and Researcher into Locational Theory and Bioinformatics
- Tomoko Nakamura, Biochemist
- Takeshi Yōrō, Anatomist
- Kyūyō Ishikawa, Writer
- Shigeru Saka, Esteemed friend of 30 years and Architect
- Sōoku Sen, Tea Ceremony Master
- Taku Satō, Designer
- Kenryū Nakamura, Professor at the Research Centre for Advanced Chemical Technology, University of Tokyo
- Kyōhei Sakaguchi, Artist
- Koichiro Kokubun, Philosopher
- Takeshi Nakajima, Political Scientist
- Kōhei Saitō, Philosopher and Marx Specialist
- Naoto Fukusawa, Product Designer and Director of the Japan Folk Art Museum

The future of one soup and one side dish

- Keiko Yamamoto, Professor of Aesthetics, Tokyo Zokei University
- Hideko Nagura, Professor at the Department of Health and Nutrition, Jumonji Gakuen Women's University

What I learnt from my conversations with them was that, if I took food as the basis for their theories, I could relate to what they were saying and understand what they meant. Naturally, they were all sympathetic when they found out what I wanted to talk about, and I was able to share my ideas. At the end of the day, cooking is connected to the earth. Cooking – this small and familiar task that humans do – must work in tandem with the earth. The ancient Japanese spirit that symbolises Japanese culture acknowledges and feels the world in which many different lives co-exist, and there is no antagonism there. 'Mono no aware', our sadness at the fleeting nature of things, hurts us in different ways, and the work of scientists is to address this by trying to find out the things we do not know. This suddenly became clear to me. I think that now, partly as a result of this book, many people have come to realise that maybe cooking should be taken more seriously. I was going up the hotel escalator

Rice, Miso Soup, Pickles

on my way to a meeting with Tessū Shaku (a Japanese Buddhist monk and religious scholar) when I realised that 'one soup and one side dish' is actually a Buddhist prayer. If you think about it like this, you will understand that life itself is an apprenticeship.

I wonder how long the Covid pandemic will go on for. I suppose nobody knows. But assuming that it will end one day, I think it will be when we notice something, understand something, change something about ourselves.

Cooking is something so familiar that perhaps nobody has thought of it in any depth before. I have never made an academic pursuit out of cooking, so I cannot say whether it is an academic discipline or not. Nevertheless, the things that cooking has led me to think all seem to be coherent. Past, future and present. The almighty sun, otentosama, the Earth, nature and the work of man are all connected in a straight line. Takeshi Nakajima was kind enough to write an essay entitled 'The Cosmology of One Soup and One Side Dish' (included in *Korona-go no Sekai*, 'The World After Covid', Chikuma Shobo, 2020). Our dietary habits based on one soup and one side dish form a cycle with the workings of the Earth. By thinking about one soup and one side dish in such depth, I

The future of one soup and one side dish

feel as if I have understood the significance of cooking and managed to come face to face with its origins for the first time.

When it was first published, I thought that with 'The Proposal That One Soup and One Side Dish Is Enough' I would be able to rediscover washoku and Japanese home cooking. In the event, rediscovering washoku meant rediscovering myself. Cooking means always becoming a new version of yourself. Nature is forever changing, so if you are using natural produce, you cannot just follow the recipe. And when you are in dialogue with an ever-changing nature, you have to renew yourself as well. You are constantly changing into a new version of yourself. This means you cannot rely on the person you were yesterday or the recipe you used yesterday. This, in turn, means it is always new: you do not even know whether you will succeed or not. If I boil spring greens in salty water and drain them, they lose their bitterness and show me their fresh, green faces. When my new self experiences something for the first time, I think, 'Look how beautiful it is,' and I am moved, no matter how many times it happens. I find countless new ways to cook things, and even when I am preparing the same dish, I can always make something new. Something different always emerges.

I feel as if I have become free in the true sense of the word. Well, I actually still have some stubborn prejudices, so perhaps there is still more potential. But I think there is hope as well as love in one soup and one side dish.

We live in a world of abundance, but I think we can all feel the signs that the Earth is in crisis and know what it could mean for humanity. Rather than continuing to paper over the cracks and making small changes just to get through, as we are doing at the moment, I think we need to go back to the beginning and have a re-set, finding as many new things, things that are different to the way they were, and new ways of doing things, as we can. I am full of hope.

I would like to take this opportunity to thank all the people who have shared their great wisdom and their many realisations with me. My profound thanks to all of you.

September 2021
Yoshiharu Doi

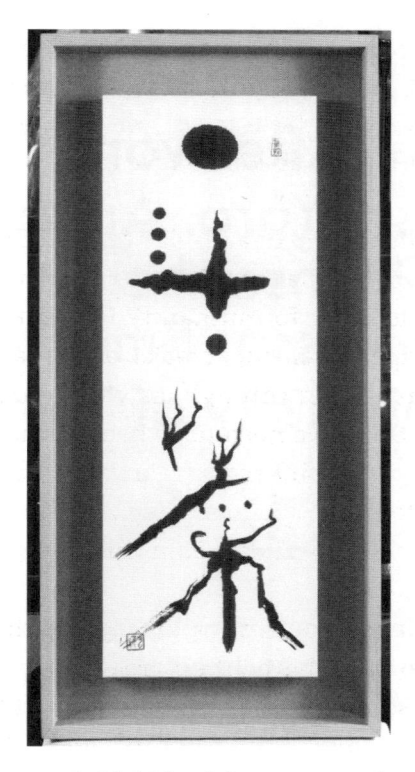

The Japanese words ichijū issai ('one soup and one side dish'), given to me by Kyūyō Ishikawa.

Afterword
Takeshi Yōrō, Anatomist, Philosopher and Professor Emeritus, University of Tokyo

When I think of Yoshiharu Doi, the word 'clean-cut' comes to mind. In his behaviour, his everyday appearance, his way of cooking, the way he writes, there is no excessive ornament – it is all crisp and clean. He has spent decades of his life on cooking; he is the epitome of someone who has devoted himself to his craft. But he has not confined himself to the kitchen, far from it. He can discuss the whole of creation, and his deep knowledge of Japanese culture, which he considers through the medium of a Japanese cuisine that is built on the senses, is unrivalled.

Afterword

The title of this book was always going to be 'The Proposal That One Soup and One Side Dish Is Enough.' It is a proposal, nothing more. You could also call it 'an individual's conviction', but he chose a humbler expression, and this is a perfect illustration of his character. His words stand in stark contrast to the pronouncements of those politicians who declare that 'greenhouse gas emissions must be reduced to zero by the year 20--!' His peaceful but realistic insistence is that we change not only our daily lives, but the world. I believe we can too. The last part of the book *Kurashi no Tame no Ryōrigaku* ('Culinary Studies for Living', NHK, 2021), by the same author, is titled 'One Soup and One Side Dish Is Like a Buddhist Prayer', and indeed, the consistency of the author's attitude can be glimpsed throughout this book too.

I am really only interested in food because of Yoshiharu Doi. When I watch gourmet cookery shows on television, they just make me angry. Japan's defeat in the Second World War occurred when I was in my second year of primary school. I belong to the generation that survived food shortages both during and after the war. I still prefer not to eat pumpkins and sweet potatoes. Young people often tell me, 'My granny feels the same way,' and this always gives me a queer feeling, both happy and sad. I wonder what sort of memory this kind of food hatred should be classified as. I studied some neurology in my later years, but I still do not understand why it is necessary for the brain to store the thought that 'I do not want to eat pumpkin or sweet potato,' in some form in some part of my brain for decades. 'One soup' refers to miso soup, but we had no miso in those days anyway. So-called seasonings like miso, soy sauce and sugar, etc. had completely disappeared. A premise for the model referred to as 'one soup and one side dish' is the existence of rice, but I still do not have the sense that rice is my staple food. I am fine not having rice for 3 days or so, and from about the third day, I start to think, 'Come to think of it, I haven't had any rice for a while, maybe I should try and have some soon.'

This is a gentle book in all sorts of different ways. Even the style in which it is written is easy. What goes on the dining table is an everyday matter, no special effort is needed to understand it. Lofty ideals are not required. Doi puts the reader's mind at ease with the message that they can just go about their lives in a straightforward way. This is also a kind of 'gentleness'. If you recite '*Namu Amida Butsu*' (a Buddhist prayer meaning 'I Take Refuge in Amida Buddha,' expressing gratitude and faith), then sooner or later you will die in the land of Pure Bliss. Towards the end

Afterword

of the first section, 'Food is our daily life', Doi says, 'What is important in daily life is where you rest your heart: to create a daily pattern which involves returning home to a comfortable place every day.' I call this the 'philosophy of self-sufficiency'. Or, to put it another way, 'The cat's way of life.' The cat will go to the most comfortable place in the house, curl up and go to sleep there. In the human world, people who cannot be self-sufficient tend to complain about this and that. They add to the existing number of rules, turning the world into an annoying place. Doi tells us that food is the basis of life, so you should probably start by becoming self-sufficient. I think this is an eminently gentle, reasonable argument; it is also easy to implement.

Doi's ideas remind me of the anecdote about Toyotomi Hideyoshi, someone who rose from a peasant background to become one of the most powerful men in Japanese history, being the sandal-bearer to Oda Nobunaga, who was often regarded as the first 'great unifier' of Japan. It is a philosophy about taking over the world from humble beginnings. I do not think that sandal-bearer Hideyoshi was originally intending to take over Japan. But I believe that if we adopt Doi's philosophy, it might become a way to help a world that is suffering due to global warming. In the

Book of Rites, a classic of Confucianism, it says that those who wish to rule the land must first cultivate their own characters. The idea of transforming the world by starting with the way you eat is surely just this: one soup and one side dish is the first step in cultivating one's own character.

September 2021

Glossary

aji	horse mackerel
akadashimiso	literally 'red stock miso'; a blended miso made from hardened soybean miso mixed with a softer kind to make it easier to use
araigome	rice that has been washed and is ready for use
arajiru	a soup made from boiling leftover fish scraps
asari	clams
ayu	sweetfish
barazushi	vinegared rice with special toppings, such as eggs, bamboo shoots, seafood and nori; also known as *chirashizushi*
bentō	a packed lunch or lunchbox
chirashizushi	see *barazushi*
daikon	a long, white radish with a mild, peppery flavour

Rice, Miso Soup, Pickles

dengaku	a style of cooking where the ingredients are grilled on skewers or simmered, and then coated with a sweet and savoury miso sauce
dobinmushi	literally, 'steamed in a teapot'; a broth steamed in an earthenware pot with matsutake mushrooms, chicken or shrimp
donburi	cooked rice, topped with various ingredients, served in a large bowl
fukinotō	the edible flower buds of the *Petasites japonicus* plant, an early spring delicacy
gobō	burdock root
gyōza	Chinese dumplings made from ground meat or vegetables wrapped in a thinly rolled piece of dough, pinched to create a seal
haré	formal, ceremonial, 'best'
ikura	salmon caviar
itadakimasu	a phrase that literally means, 'I humbly receive,' but that is a way of giving thanks to all the people involved in the production and preparation of the food one is about to eat

Glossary

junsai	water shield
kachūyu	a simple miso soup from Okinawa, made by pouring hot water over bonito flakes and miso
kaiseki	a sophisticated Japanese style of cuisine served in multiple courses
kamaboko	a steamed fish cake
karashi-su-miso	mustard miso dressing
karé raisu	gently spiced Japanese curry, typically prepared using a block of curry mix and served with rice
karomi	lightness
kasujiru	a miso soup made with sake lees
katsuobushi	simmered, smoked and fermented skipjack tuna or mackerel flakes
ke	commonplace, ordinary, everyday
kenchinjiru	a vegetable soup made with tofu fried in sesame oil
kinome	the leaf bud of a Japanese pepper tree
kireaji	a sharp, crisp and clean aftertaste
kiriboshi	daikon cut into narrow strips and dried
kōji	cooked rice that has been inoculated with a fermentation culture, *Aspergillus oryzae*

Rice, Miso Soup, Pickles

komatsuna	Japanese mustard spinach
kombu	a thick and slightly rubbery type of edible kelp
kouta	a Japanese ballad accompanied on the shamisen
kyūrimomi	cucumber that has been sliced very finely and salted to draw out the liquid before being washed and drained
maitake	hen-of-the-woods mushrooms
misoshiru	miso soup
mitsuba	Japanese chervil
mochi	dumplings or rice cakes made from pounded glutinous rice
mugitoro	barley rice topped with grated Japanese mountain yam
naberyōri	a style of cooking where meat, fish and vegetables are cooked in a hot pot, usually placed in the middle of the table, with people helping themselves straight from the pot
nabeyakiudon	a one-pot noodle soup that is a Japanese winter staple
yakinasu	grilled aubergine
niboshi	small, dried sardines

Glossary

niebana	the state of a soup or stew just after it has begun to boil
nikujaga	literally 'meat and potatoes'; a dish of meat, potatoes, carrots and onions stewed in dashi, soy sauce, mirin and sugar
nimono	food that has been stewed or simmered
nitsuke	a dish where the vegetables are first fried then boiled in a sauce containing sake, mirin, sugar and soy sauce
nori	dried edible seaweed (a form of red algae)
nukazuke	pickles made in brine and fermented rice bran
oden	a stew consisting of fish cakes, boiled eggs, daikon radish and other things simmered in a light broth
ohagi	sweet rice balls coated in tsubuan
ohitashi	literally, 'something soaked'; a style of cooking vegetables where they are blanched and soaked in a dashi-based sauce
okayu	a porridge made with rice and water
okazu	side dish

Rice, Miso Soup, Pickles

onigiri	balls of steamed rice compressed into a triangular or cylindrical shape, often wrapped in nori seaweed and prepared with a variety of savoury fillings
osechi ryōri	special dishes that are cooked in advance and eaten to celebrate the New Year
ozōni	Japanese New Year's soup made with mochi and vegetables
renkon	lotus root
sansai	edible wild plants
sanshō	Japanese pepper, a spice with a citrusy, peppery flavour
sashimi	thinly sliced raw fish or seafood, often eaten with soy sauce
satoimo	Japanese taro
shiohigari	literally, 'low tide gathering'; clamming
shirumono	soup
sōmen	very thin noodles made from wheat flour
sudachi	a small green citrus fruit with a tart, acidic taste
suimono	a delicate, transparent Japanese soup, literally 'something you sip'

Glossary

suiton	small flour dumplings
sukiyaki	a hot pot made with meat and vegetables, simmered in a broth of soy sauce, sugar and mirin
sukkiri	clean and refreshing
sunomono	literally 'vinegared things'; any dish seasoned with vinegar, but typically a cucumber salad
takikomi gohan	seasoned steamed rice with meat and vegetables
takuan	a pickled daikon radish with a crunchy texture and a sweet and tangy flavour
tempura	a style of cooking vegetables and seafood where they are coated in a thin batter and deep fried
teriyaki	a style of cooking where the ingredients are grilled with a glaze of soy sauce, mirin and sugar
tonjiru	a hearty kind of miso soup made with slices of pork belly and a variety of vegetables
tsubuan	coarse sweet red bean paste
tsukemono	pickles
tsukeshōyū	soy sauce, mirin and sake

Rice, Miso Soup, Pickles

tsukudani	preserved food boiled in soy
udo	*Aralia cordata*
udon	thick noodles made from wheat flour
umeboshi	sour and salty pickled plums
wakame	a thin and silky type of edible kelp
washoku	Japanese cuisine
yudōfu	tofu cooked in stock and served with various condiments, such as grated ginger, spring onions and soy sauce
yuzu	a spherical, yellow citrus fruit with a complex flavour; a Japanese citron
zarusoba	chilled buckwheat noodles served in a bamboo basket with dipping sauce and various toppings
zōsui	a mild and comforting Japanese rice soup or rice porridge, made with vegetables, eggs and meat or fish

Index

Page numbers in *italic* refer to the illustrations

A
Aichi 68
Ainu 154
Akizuki, Dr Ichirō 46, 62
alcohol 27
amberjack 217
araigome (prepared rice) 59–61
Asuka period 152
aubergines 74, 76, 211
autumn 213–15
autumn miso soup 75–6
avidyā (spiritual ignorance) 41

B
bacteria 59, 61, 71, 138
bamboo shoots 209–10, 211, 225–8
barazushi (scattered sushi) 26
barley miso 69, 70
beans 210
beauty 165–8, 220–1
bitter tastes 10, 130–1, 139, 142, 208–9
blood sugar levels 178–9
Book of Rites 256
brain 15–16, 145, 254
bran, rice 58–9
bread 86–7, 169, 176, 178
Brillat-Savarin, Jean Anthelme 49
Brussels sprouts 217
Buddha 142, 163
Buddhism 41, 148, 247, 254
buds 208–9

C

calcium 56, 64, 73
calmness 15–16
calories 173, 176
capitalism 40
ceremonial food 25–8
chain restaurants 108–10
chefs, professional 95–7, 105–8, 128
chestnuts 213
children 4–5, 43–5, 48–9, 97–9, 102–4, 113–16, 121–2, 160–1, 193–4
China 138, 140, 171, 184–7, 189
Chinese cabbage 215–16
chirashizushi (scattered sushi) 26, 186
chopsticks 152–3, 162, 193, 195, 234
Christmas 161
circular farming 175
clams 74, 77–8
cleanliness 150, 151–5, 162, 181–2
climate 10–11, 32–3, 47
climate change 255–6
comfort 15
confectionery 134
Confucianism 256
constitution 46–7

convenience foods 47, 110, 173–4
cookery schools 175
cooking
  ceremonial food 25–8
  post-war period 170–1
  professional cooking 95–7, 105–10
  significance of 37–41
  see also home cooking
cooking schools 170
Covid pandemic 241, 247
craftsmen 167
cravings 18

D

daikon radish 16, 23–4, 216
daily life 30–2, 37–40
deep-fried food 170, 174
deliciousness 15–17
digestive system 9, 144
discernment 117–23
dishes 220
Doi, Masaru 160
'Dual Language Nation Japan' 27–8, 184–6
dumplings 84–5

E

E. coli 71

early humans 9–10, 143–50, 151, 152, 154
earthenware 145, 146–7
eating 37–9, 49–50
eggs, in miso soup 66
emotions 48, 119, 130
Europe 10
everyday pleasure 193–4
evolution 144

F
'family restaurants' 174, 175
famines 146
farming 57, 175
fast food 174
fat 56, 63, 173
feelings 48
fermented foods *see* miso; pickles
fire 143–4, 146
fish 78–9, 139, 153–4, 171–2, 200, 210
flavours 56, 70
flounder 102–3
food poisoning 71
food preparation 23–4, 37
fruit 33, 163
'frying pan movement' 170, 174

G
gardens 30–2, 231, 232
gingko nuts 214–15
Gishiwajinden 151
global warming 255–6
gods 25–6, 151, 207
gorillas 42–3, 144
gourmet restaurants 107

H
Hakozaki, Noriko 232–5
hands 228–9
haré (ceremonial) 25, 131, 179
Hashimoto, Mari 243–4
Hatchō miso 69, 70–1
health 46, 175–6
hearing 134–5
Hideyoshi, Toyotomi 255
Hiroshima 70
Hokkaido 233
home cooking 21–4, 25
  aims 93–4, 97–9
  children and 41, 102–4, 111–16
  and innovation 101
  recognition of 128–9
Horigome, Yoshio 223–8
hot pots 147–8
hygiene 27, 141

I

Ikoma 232–3
illness 176, 239–40
innovation, home cooking 101
Ise Shrine, Mie Prefecture 32
Ishikawa, Kyūyō 27–8, 184–5, 251

J

Japanese pepper plant 209
Japaneseness 182–7
Jōmon period 143–50, 151, 152, 154, 237

K

Kagawa 70, 85
kaiseki cuisine 23
Kansai region 70, 83–4
ke (commonplace) 25, 131, 179
'kitchen cars' 170, 174
Kobayashi, Tatsuo 146, 237
Korean barbecue 138, 177
kouta (ballad) 29
Kumoda, Minoru 230–1, 232
Kyoto 69, 85
Kyoto University 42
Kyūshū miso 69, 70

L

lactobacilli 71
language 185
leisure 198–9
life stages 43–4
living beautifully 223–7
love 44, 101, 118, 198, 202

M

mackerel pike 213
main dishes 171–3
markets 33
meal cycle 38–9, *38*
mealtimes 162
meat 63–4, 130, 147, 162, 169, 171–3
Meiji period 184–5
microorganisms 8–9, 10
milk 169
minerals 56, 63, 172
miso 8
  decline in consumption 176
  flavours 70
  miso paste 63, 68–71
  power of 71
miso soup 6, 67, 72, 231, 237–8
  appearance 68
  cooking 72–3
  for one person 64–5

'one soup and one side
    dish' philosophy 5,
    55–6
  in practice 82–5
  seasonal soups 73–7
  stock 79–81
  with fish 78–9
  with lots of ingredients
    62–8
  with seafood 74, 77–9
mochi rice 216
mono no aware
    (impermanence of
    things) 167–8, 182–3, 247
Motoori, Norinaga 167, 183,
    230
mushrooms 63, 76, 214, 230

N

Nagasaki 46
Nakajima, Takeshi 247
nameko mushrooms 9
nature 9, 10–11, 57, 151, 223–5,
    236–7, 245–6
New Year 26, 85, 197, 208,
    216
Nobunaga, Oda 255
noodles 80, 187–8
nutrition 171–2, 177–9
nutritional deficiencies 169

O

octopus 9
oil 170, 174, 186–7
Oka, Kiyoshi 40, 41, 48
okazu (side dishes) 55
okayu 239
Okinawa 72, 233
'one soup and one side dish'
    5, 6, 7–8, 55–6
  importance of 245–50
  in practice 82–5
  reactions to the book
    241–4
  as style of eating 86–9, 89
Osaka 28–9, 100, 179, 195–6
Osaka World Expo 174, 175
osechi (special dishes) 26
otentosama (watchful sun)
    148–9, 152, 183, 229–30,
    247

P

pasta 86, 178
peace of mind 45
peas 210
peppers 211
pickles 6, 55–6, 212, 215–16
pleasing your family
    200–3
potato drop soup 76

processed food 8, 21–2, 47, 93
professional cooking 95–7, 105–10
protein 56, 63, 169, 173
pumpkin 75

R
rainfall 32
ramen 173–4, 175, 187–8
restaurants 93, 95–7, 100, 105–10, 117–18, 174, 175, 201, 241
rice 6, 8, 57–61
  cooking 58–61, *58*
  decline in consumption 169, 176
  farming 57–8
  names 58
  nutritional benefits 56
  okayu 239
  'one soup and one side dish' 55–6
  taste 139
  in tea ceremony 131–2
rice bowls 121, 195–7, *197*
rice bran 58–9
rice cookers 60
rice miso 68, 70
rice mochi 216
root vegetables 77

S
Saikyō miso 69–70
sake 207, 221
salmon roe 214
salt 5, 27
sashimi 27, 133–4, 153–4
Satō, Taku 237–9
school lunches 174
sculpture 142
sea bream 78
seafood, miso soup with 74, 77–9
seasonal eating 73–7, 129, 132, 146, 163, 207–18
seaweed 16, 63, 74
Second World War 171, 253
security 15
self-sufficiency 255
Sendai miso 69
senses 119–20, 131–42
Shaku, Tessū 247
shellfish 154, 210
Shimizu, Hiroshi 99, 118–19
shinjin kyōshoku (gods and people eating together) 26
Shinshū miso 69, 70
Shinto 32
shopping 159–60
shrines 32, 163

Index

side dishes 55, 89, *89*, 132, 172–3
sight 133–4
smell, sense of 137–8
social media 21, 96, 178
solar terms 208
soups 148, 153
   see also miso soup
sour tastes 212
Soviet Union 173
soybean miso 68–9, 70–1
spinach 216
spring 208–10
spring miso soup 73–4
steamed rice 58–61, *58*
stews 64, 148
stock 62, 79–81
summer 210–12
summer miso soup 74–5
sushi 23, 26, 165, 177
Suzuki, Ichirō 18–19, 179

T

takeaway food 159–60
Tanaka, Ikko 231–2, 238
taro 75–6, 214
taste, sense of 137, 138–42, 219
tea ceremony 29, 119, 131–2, 135, 138, 148, 186, 202–3, 232, 245–6

temperature 65, 136–7
Teresa, Mother 50
textures 136–7
tofu 63, 133–4, 165–6, 215
Tokyo 233, 241
Tokyo Olympics (1964) 175
tomatoes 163
touch, sense of 135–7
trays 204–6
tsukemono see pickles

U

udon noodles 80
umami flavours 139, 142
UNESCO 127–9, 185–6, 187–8
United States of America 169–71, 173

V

value of food 115
value systems 27–8
vegetables 6, 33, 63, 130–1, 139, 172
vitamins 56, 63, 172

W

wakame seaweed 74
wasabi 22
washoku (Japanese cuisine) 27, 93, 127–9, 142, 245, 249

waste 140–1
water
  miso soup 63, 66
  in nature 223–5
  steaming rice 60
water dropwort 209
water shield 211
watermelon 163
Western cuisine and culture 22–3, 86–7, 137, 138, 140, 161, 162, 171, 184–5, 187 189, 245

winter 215–17
winter miso soup 77
Wrangham, Richard 144

Y
Yakimono Ikoma 232–5
Yamagiwa, Juichi 42–3
Yanagi, Muneyoshi 149, 245
Yōrō, Takeshi 252–6

Z
Zaccheroni, Alberto 22